"This is a beautifully honest and thought-provoking account of the physical and mental struggles of living with a long term chronic illness such as Long Covid; the uncertainty for the future, the feeling of being isolated from the world, and the sheer depths to which we can fall whilst suffering. This memoir embraces and accepts all of the dark, and yet still allows the light to shine through."

– Jackie Baxter, *Long Covid Podcast*

"Sensitive and revealing...Skyeris' writing is clear, authentic, and deeply human throughout, often expressing her ideas and reactions in emotionally charged sentences that convey the intensity and confusion of the pandemic era. A searing, deeply personal memoir of chronic illness."

– *Kirkus Reviews*

still

moving

Skyeris

First edition 2023

Cover design by Hazel Lam
Text design by Peter Long
Author photo by Emerald Dove

Paperback ISBN 979-8-9893539-0-3
Ebook ISBN 979-8-989-3539-1-0

www.skyeris.art

- for Mudflower & the crew -

contents

contents

forewords

As of writing this, it's been nearly four years to the day that a man dismissed my symptoms as resistance to meditation. You'll get that story in the earliest pages, gentle reader, so I won't continue it here.

This work is an attempt to capture the first three years of my psycho-spiritual experience of SARS-CoV-2. This is a personal story, about a specific illness now called Long Covid, and those with it called long-haulers. That ~~said~~ written, many moments in my Long Covid experience are also true for the broader experience of living with chronic illness.

If you live with chronic illness, I hope these pages validate and provide insight into your experience. If you don't live with chronic illness, I hope these pages illuminate struggles that are too often invisible or invalidated.

This book is not a log of my symptoms, not a medical record of stats and patterns. Nor is it a diagnostic tool or reference for Long Covid. Rather, it is an account of my intensely visceral experience. In reading, you will encounter many facets of that intensity, so please consider this your

CN[1] for illness, ideation, relationship struggles, and other difficult subjects.

Nor is it a neat, steady narrative. The timing and pacing are inconsistent, which reflects the dissolved time of those years.

~~Speaking~~ Typing of time, you might have noticed that this book begins in 2019. Covid was not widely known until 2020, which means that when I first fell ill, I was without the full context. I was an early adopter, albeit unwillingly and unknowingly.

Since then, the combination of blurry memories and cultural amnesia and overwhelming global events has rendered the recollection of significant moments and developments foggy for many people. For this reason, this book has an appendix, with relevant resources, and a selected timeline.

In the first year and a half of my Long Covid experience, I didn't want to talk about it. When I finally did, I hated it—so much so that I regretted saying anything at all, and I stopped.

Eventually, though, many caring, thoughtful people in my life started asking me to share. I was grateful for their genuine interest in my health. I still didn't want to talk about

---

1 Content Notice = advance notice of intense, sensitive topics. In this space, honesty begins at the beginning. CN for Covid, Long Covid, chronic illness, chronic pain, ideation (throughout). Additionally, in 2021, CN for murder and suicide. Please do not continue reading if you tend to be on the edge of harming yourself or others. Please do not continue reading if you're in a delicate space and might get overwhelmed. Please take exquisite care of yourself.

Long Covid. But I also wanted to answer honestly, and I couldn't condense my katabasis into a few paragraphs.

Which led me to writing about it, which was another thing I didn't want to do. I never wanted to give words to this experience. Never wanted to imbue life into it, via language.

But all that not-sharing revealed that if I didn't write this, one day I would start screaming...and not stop.

I wrote this because I needed to make mental and emotional space. To clear out the cobwebby muck (more of that later as well), so that I can do other things. And to share once, for whomever is curious, rather than tell this story repeatedly—a task which I know, in my marrow, I cannot do.

Instead of waiting until I'm "cured," I decided to share about the three years after my first symptoms appeared. The story is ongoing. Life continues to emerge. Life itself—ever indefatigable—reasserts its inevitability.

2019

I sat quietly on the ground, while the meditation teacher barely looked at me. Chin down, I didn't stop the tears falling into my lap and onto the grass. I struggled to steady my shaking breaths in the gentle heat and humidity of a tropical autumn, and focused on not fainting.

I was ashamed. Ashamed, and angry at myself for that shame, given that nothing warranted it. And yet, his disinterest made me feel like a failure. I was ashamed about all of it.

In early November 2019, on the first day of a silent meditation retreat, I began exhibiting flu-like symptoms: fever, congestion, body ache, headache. I'd hoped that the meditation retreat would also feel like a semi-vacation. I was two flights away from home, across a continent and halfway across an ocean, and had surrendered my phone at the start of the retreat.

That first night, I slept poorly, restless on the cot in my tent, hoping I'd feel better in the morning. I hated the idea of telling anyone, but I was also skeptical of my capacity to participate.

And for good reason: the next morning, I nearly passed out in the first session. So I told the retreat manager, who told the meditation teacher. Rather than engaging with me directly—or asking any questions—he spoke to the manager, dismissing my experience as an adverse reaction to intensive meditation practice. He told her, loudly enough for me to hear, that my symptoms were common among people resisting the rigors of meditation.

In other words: I was having a tantrum.

I disagreed, but I had no residual energy to advocate for myself, to point out that I'd been meditating regularly for over a decade. Instead, while my tears spilled onto my lap and the grass, the gentle heat and humidity of that tropical autumn felt smothering.

Meanwhile, the retreat manager convinced the meditation teacher to allow me to rest for one session, then rejoin the group. I nodded my thanks to her and stumbled into my tent. I was worried about myself, but I was equally concerned about contagion for the other participants. Even if the meditation teacher didn't care about them, I did. One of them was pregnant.

I slept for a couple of hours and felt worse. When I found the retreat manager after my nap, she said the meditation teacher insisted that I return to all the sessions. No more resting. Not even for the remainder of the day, with my fervent hope that I had a 24-hour flu and would feel fine the next day.

"No, he won't allow you to miss that much time," she

explained sympathetically. "I'll set up your space for the next session."

In a flash, I found the strength to advocate for myself. "Understood," I replied. While she nodded, I continued, "I'm leaving. I'll start packing; please bring my phone to me right away. I'll be gone in an hour."

Her jaw dropped, and I didn't wait for her to recover her composure. I knew it wasn't her fault, but I was too upset to play polite.

And too distraught to tell her how upset I was. I had been so excited for this retreat, which was focused on women in leadership. Earlier in the year, I'd quit all my work and creative collaborations—things I thought I'd be doing for decades. In my grief, I was inspired to apply to the retreat, in the hopes of a new start.

Given the competition for the few spaces, I doubted the acceptance of my application. I was ecstatic when I received the invitation; this would be the refresh I desperately wanted. I had confidence that the coming years would be my best, with my best work and my best art. I was proud of this fresh start, that I'd exited toxic work settings and toxic relationships. I was ready for a wide open future.

Again I stumbled into my tent, in a haze of tears, devastated to leave so soon. Compared to the travel time from home to the retreat location, I'd barely been at the retreat longer than my time in transit.

Despite the disbelief from the meditation teacher, I knew I wasn't having an adverse reaction to a rigorous meditation schedule. I was hoping for a one-day flu, and I was frustrated that I had to leave, simply to take the most basic care of myself. Moreover, I felt guilty that someone else missed the opportunity to attend the entire ten-day retreat, since I was leaving on the second day.

Reception at the retreat property was enough for texts, but not phone calls. Even before I had my phone, even within the limited options at that moment, I already had a plan and contingency plans.[1] I hoped that my partner would be available to find somewhere for me to stay, and then we could discuss what to do next. I wasn't completely confident, only because of the time difference. He could be in the metro on the way home from work, or perhaps had plans with friends after work.

I knew one person on the island. Before the retreat, we'd discussed the possibility me visiting for a few days, after the retreat ended. But I didn't know her that well, so I was reluctant to spring a big change in timing.

Outside of those plans, I could simply walk off the retreat property. With my backpack, onto a rural road, in the heat, until I reached better reception. That option was far from ideal, even if I'd not been sick. But it was a terrible choice, given that I could barely walk straight without my backpack.

---

1   My work background includes experience in logistics and event management. Whenever I decide something, my default setting has already considered multiple scenarios, safety concerns, liability, consequences (expected and unexpected), execution, challenges, course corrections, and more. I know how to plan.

And yet, that was my backup plan. Far from my preference, but I was spitting mad and thus willing, if needed, to opt for bravado that was a lot more stagger than swagger.

Luckily for me, my partner was working late and received my terse texts:

> i'm leaving the course early
> everything is fine, but too complicated
> for text explanation
> i'll be free to talk later
> i also don't have wifi. will you see
> if there's a room at the hostel near
> the airport? last time i stayed in an
> economy single
> if not there, would prefer something
> with restaurants or commercial area
> nearby

A few hours later, I reached the hotel room my partner booked. Although I desperately wanted to sleep, I knew he was anxious to know the reason for my departure. He had no idea what had happened to me—if I had fallen ill, been sexually assaulted (oh, that definitely happens, more than you might think), or something worse.

I called, and we discussed whether I should change my ticket and come home earlier. Beyond my doubts that I'd manage the travel alone, I was still concerned about contagion for others. I wished going home was the best option;

staying on the island seemed like a terrible option. As much as I was reluctant to ask my friend, Laney, to stay with her, that seemed to be for the best.

First, though, I laid in bed, in the hopes of mustering the strength to walk to a nearby grocery store. After a restless nap, I walked slowly, so as not to trip on flat ground. At the grocery, I stocked up on some fruit and nuts, pre-made food, and a few nonalcoholic drinks. The walk home with a backpack of groceries was even slower.

Back in my room, I called Laney, unable to postpone the conversation. I told her everything: that I didn't have the budget to spend nearly two weeks in hotels or hostels. That I was certain that going home early would make me sicker, not to mention the likelihood of infecting others.

And, of course, that staying with her would put her at risk. Ever generous, she didn't rescind the invitation. She was actually very enthusiastic about an earlier and longer visit, and we agreed to be very careful about shared spaces in her home, to reduce contagion.

By twilight, I was already asleep. Still full of false bravado, I'd told myself that I'd feel fine in the morning.

The next morning I felt worse; I wanted to sleep all day. But I'm stubborn, and I hate feeling unwell. So I dragged myself out of bed, rolled out my mat, and started what I thought would be a short pranayama and asana[2] practice, my usual thing when I'm away from home. In all, about

---

2   pranayama = breathwork; asana = posture

fifteen minutes.

My body felt like wet cement, with agility to match. My "short" practice took forty-five minutes, as I struggled mightily to breathe.

Fortunately, I'd requested a late checkout. Following a quick shower, I called Laney, afraid that she'd changed her mind. I wouldn't have blamed her. She confirmed that an imminent arrival wasn't inconvenient, and I got a rideshare.

Her home was a paradise spot, in a small cleared space amidst the jungle, on a hill overlooking the ocean. I dropped my backpack and sat in a chair in the yard, savoring the sunshine and the breeze. I still felt awful, but I was grateful to find a moment of peace.

In my own body, however, the nearly two weeks with her was far from peaceful. I was constantly tormented by a hacking cough and was so congested I could barely smell anything. Typical in my history of respiratory ailments.

And though I'd coughed and sneezed my way through any number of colds, flus, and other respiratory issues, this sickness was different. It...shocked me. Never had I woken up at night because I was coughing and hacking with such force that sleep became impossible. Never did I have to take so many breaks doing simple tasks and ordinary movements, like walking on a level path. Never had I been so exhausted by the mere fact of having my eyes open. I wanted to lie in bed and sleep all day, every day. Not surprising, given that I was hacking more than sleeping through the night.

My partner, who likewise had never witnessed me this ill, was also concerned. He knew about my history with respiratory issues. I wasn't panicking, and he seemed to mirror my perspective.

What he didn't know was that my calm wasn't for lack of cause, but from exhaustion. I wanted to do nothing, all the time. Be still. Be quiet. From years of living with migraines and a childhood heavily punctuated by respiratory issues, though, I knew those struggles are less severe when I am not still. Movement is, quite literally for me, the difference between living versus simply existing.

On all levels, health is a function of movement. Circulation, which passes chemical messages all over the body. The pulses of CSF.[3] Endless heartbeats. The nature of the universe is movement. Tides, seasons. Galaxies spinning, stars exploding and rebirthing. Quantum movement exists in the coldest, stillest temperatures. Even light and sound come to us through movement: they travel to us, through us, beyond us.

I persisted. Still moving. Despite the lack of sleep, the bombardment of headaches, the endless congestion. Springs bubbling. Still moving.

Nearly two weeks in the island paradise—which, lest you think it was a luxury vacation, had no indoor bathroom, and barely any phone or internet connection—was an ideal setting to keep moving. The view and the wildlife—steady tides, lush foliage, outrageous flowers, fresh fruit, constant

---

3   cerebrospinal fluid

birdsong— were more than enough luxury for me.

At the time, I was fifteen years into a consistent meditation, breathwork, and postural practice. I'd practiced in beautiful studio spaces, but also muddy fields. Airports, grimy hotel rooms, abandoned rooftops, tiny hallways. On mild, beautiful mornings, but also on frigid mornings wearing a coat. When my body felt fantastic, but also when I had a cold or headaches or heatstroke and even with a fractured arm. This is not to say I reflect on these choices and think they were all for the best. But they are an easy way to show my commitment to what matters to me.

While on the island I continued my practice, not missing a day, though each one was like that morning in the hotel. I needed triple or quadruple the time, mostly to cough and blow my nose and rest between sun salutations. The same happened in my meditation practice. Stating the obvious: hacking is not conducive to sitting quietly and trying to clear the mind.

I was desperate to believe that I was overreacting. I tried to convince myself that I couldn't truly be as sick as I felt. Throughout my life, I have made scores of decisions in order to stay as healthy as possible. I don't smoke. I barely drink. One year I had six drinks total, in the entire year, and I was shocked at my high consumption. I had never been this sick, ever.

My denial justified exhausting myself, trying to prove things weren't really that bad. I took long, slow walks in the jungle, in vegetation so thick that I lost the nearby ocean completely to sight and nearly completely to sound. In those moments, consumed by trees and vines and birdsong and breeze, I questioned mySelf. Was I exaggerating? Dreaming? I questioned the universe too. Was I delusional? What was happening?

Several times, I visited a series of small waterfalls and pools, where I dangled my feet in crisp, cool water. This spot had a much taller cataract going off a cliff. My first time there, I gazed at the water tumbling over the edge. On subsequent visits, I sidled closer to the edge, where the thick vegetation below prevented seeing the bottom. I wanted to see beyond. As I leaned to peer further, I realized that I'd topple over the edge and disappear into the jungle. I took a shuddering breath, stepped back, then laid on the rocks before creeping towards the view again.

I also managed a couple trail walks to the shore. The downhill was steep enough that I needed to rest at the beach. The uphill was so steep that I rested for the remainder of the day.

Meanwhile, the coughing became an increasing concern. My throat felt raw all the time; my vocal cords felt shredded. During the day, my friend was at work and I was glad to be alone, with no need to talk.

In the evening, I was glad not to be alone, after so many hours with my fears and worries. Laney and I cooked dinner together several times. For the few restaurant visits, we chose places outdoors or nearly empty. We checked out books from the library.

My favorite excursion was watching sea turtles come ashore, to sleep on the beach. I was mesmerized. Not just at the sight, but also the smell. I'd never thought about the smell of the deep sea, but the turtles brought it to me. It made me think of thick moss in a forest, just the marine version. Something briny, deep, primordial.

The wildest thing I did was attempt to surf. Laney knew that I'd always wanted to try, and I downplayed my inner despair that it would be too much for me. It had taken more than forty years to try surfing, and I refused to pass on the opportunity.

If this seems unbelievable, that's understandable. I learned to disregard my pain during childhood, when I started having migraines. No one—absolutely no one—took my pain seriously. Mind you, I didn't have the language: despite me saying it frequently, "I have a headache, a really, really bad headache" did not trip anyone's awareness. Including my own. The only examples I had of migraines were "old" housewives (y'know, women in their mid-thirties on TV shows, in movies, in my community) who had to lie down in dark rooms for days.

Language is powerful, so much so that it builds reality. When something can't be expressed in words, people often can't understand. I didn't know to take my pain seriously. Instead, I simply followed the lead of adults who dismissed my struggle. That meant I went to school, finished my homework, participated in extracurriculars, did my chores, and held a job. I trained, unwittingly, how to function—barely—with migraines.

This functioning requires extreme compartmentalization and dissociation. But one copes how one copes. Three decades later, I chose dissociation in order to attempt to surf.

So, the one and only time I tried surfing, I spent most of the time pushing the board away from shore, into the tide. Not even paddling, just trudging in chest-deep water against the waves. The seabed was lined with rough rocks, and my feet bled freely from cuts. I had thin scars on both feet for over a year after that day. One scar is still visible.

In a miraculous moment, I managed to catch a wave and stand, just for a few seconds. The wave yanked me back into my body: I felt my wet feet on the board, the shimmering pain in my head, the sunlight on my eyelashes, the churn of the tide propelling me forward, the salty breeze on my skin. In those seconds, I savored the exhilaration of energy, force, power, and transcendence, all moving from the moon to the sea to me.

I realized, that day, that my unexpected time in this beautiful place was actually the best thing that could have happened to me, even while I was so sick. I had been held so lovingly, not because I'm exceptional and received something unordinary, but because this place, simply in its existence, was so nourishing. The land, the sea, the wind, the wildlife all had so much medicine.

What I didn't realize that day was that it was the last big inspiration, the last magical moment I'd have for a long, long time.

I returned home in mid-November, still terribly ill. The rest of the year was a blur, partly because I always find the holidays exhausting. That year had the added layers of incessant hacking, frequent napping, sluggish asana and pranayama practice. I hacked to the point of gagging, and often nearly dry heaving. My migraines became more frequent, which I attributed to the holidays, because I generally find them stressful.

Beyond all my desires for doubt and denial, I finally admitted to myself that I had contracted a strange illness. I knew, in my marrow, that something was seriously wrong with me.

Little did I know, then, how right I was. Though it's probably for the best that I couldn't foretell the future.

By January 2020, I was concerned. I was also still moving. Dolphins leaping, whales singing.

But I was still coughing all the time, now frequently to the point of dry heaving. The coughing had so much force that I worried my voice would be damaged for the rest of my life. It seemed the most likely scenario. My vocal cords felt as though they were in tatters.

All that coughing meant I still needed over half an hour for less than fifteen minutes of pranayama and asana. It was discouraging, and I didn't want to do it. But I knew if I stopped moving, I would disappear.

While I wasn't as congested as before, I was still hacking a lot of phlegm. This phlegm, however, was unlike anything my body had ever hacked. It was grey, and grainy. Of all the weird and gross things my body has shed from injury and illness, hacking what seemed like cobwebs was by far the grossest. I had more cobwebs than a giant, haunted attic.

In February, when the worst (but not all) of the coughing and the worst (but not all) of the sinus pressure had abated, I wondered whether to go to the doctor for blood work. I'd had cancer scares before[1] and I'd certainly just endured the strangest, most physically intense illness of my life. That seemed to warrant a doctor visit.

And—and, and, and and and—I have a difficult history with allopathic (otherwise known as conventional Western) medicine. Most of it stems from medical professionals ignoring or downplaying concerns I've expressed throughout my life: from passing out due to menstrual pain to living with migraines. What I always hoped to find was sympathy, support, and insight, in addition to genuine healing. Instead, I received pushes for pharmaceuticals or invasive interventions, with zero discussion about side effects.

(Mind you, this is not hate on all of allopathic medicine all the time. The bias against women and other marginalized[2] people is well documented; I can vouch for my experiences of that bias.)

All that to ~~say~~ write: I didn't go to the doctor. I'd like to have a more comfortable relationship with allopathic medicine, but I don't.

Because it's easy, and often likely, to feel ashamed of yourself and not trust your assessment of your own life when professionals tell you that you're lying. It's easy for children— and inevitable—to feel ashamed of themselves and not trust

---

1 Due to overzealous diagnosis, not health issues I observed. But still.

2 Marginalized populations include BIPOC, people with disabilities, LGBTQIA+ folks, women, people with chronic illness, and more.

their assessments of their own lives when adults (not just medical professionals, but also teachers, family members, and others) tell them they're lying. I've had all of this, and I've spent decades deconditioning from shame and lack of self-trust.

Meanwhile, my migraines were even worse. I've lived with migraines since before my teen years. Before 2020, a bad spell of migraines for me was a few in a month. At the start of 2020, though, I was managing them six or seven days a week. At least five.

Migraines, for me, make plenty of clichés real and reasonable. Moaning and groaning, ranting and raving. I can't lie down because a pillow or a mattress hurts my head. By that point, the air hurts. My brain feels like a mass of wires, glowing hot and searing the inside of my skull. My sinus cavities throb; my eyelids are sore; my jaw feels as tight as a vise.

I'm a synesthete, so pain registers for me beyond physical sensation. When I have headaches of any severity, I commonly see washes of color and light when I close my eyes. Those washes of color and light also register as texture in the hollows of my eyes, as if someone threw water at my face. That might sound cool and trippy and fun, but for me these layers aggravate the headache and add variations of pain.

In all, it's pain so deep that the relief of it still hurts, in its own way.

Starting in adolescence, I began using my imagination to self-soothe. Through seeing, hearing, and feeling, I have two scenarios that have soothed me for over thirty years.

(Warning: they might be super gross to you.)

One scenario is a jackhammer battering my shoulders and neck, reducing the pain to dust. The other is a meat tenderizer, pulverizing and tearing the sinew until all the pain disappears.

Yes, I understand that in reality, these tools would destroy my body. Imagination, though, allows the impossible to be real. For most of my life, imagination produced the meagerest relief from my migraines. The pain didn't end, but my imagination brought a modicum of space from the pain, space that helped me compartmentalize and dissociate.

The ongoing migraines in 2020 created ongoing, intense sleep deprivation. Because my body was in so much pain, I couldn't lie down for more than a few hours—if the pillow wasn't already too painful. That, or coughing and gagging fits would wake me up.

Certainly, the lack of sleep contributed to more frequent headaches. Sleep became elusive. I slept when I slept, which was at the whims of pain. Midnight to 3:33am. Or 5:02pm to sundown. Dawn to 11:15am. Noon to 4:58pm. And so, over the year, sleep also became illusive. The possibility of sleeping through the night, without interruption, became more and more like fantasy, something fully consigned to my past.

I lost track of days, weeks, months, seasons, time. Everyday was Today, with pain. Today, pain. Pain, today. Pain. Pain. Pain. Pain. Today. Today. Today.

Wherever, where-never. Whenever, when-never.

If you live with sleep deprivation, you know it makes everything else more difficult. If you don't live with it—sleep deprivation makes my life impossible. I can't think; I can't follow through on tasks. My temper is short. I'm too tired to give a damn. Everything is confusing.

Meanwhile, like the rest of the world in January and February 2020, I encountered, with increasing horror, the news about SARS-CoV-2.

By early March, I realized that many of my symptoms from 2019 matched this disease. Not that I did anything about it. At the time, tests were nearly impossible for non-celebrities. Months had passed since I was acutely ill, so I figured test results would be meaningless anyway. And given that I wasn't an essential worker, I didn't want to pull limited resources away from those who needed them.

And the news only worsened. Everyone who lived through March 2020 has different lasting impressions, but for me the worst was learning that Italian hospitals instituted triage protocols for the onslaught of Covid cases.[3]

And while the subsequent lockdowns were very disruptive to many people, they impacted me very little. Being sick

---

3   "Italy's health system at limit in virus-struck Lombary" by Winfield & Frances D'Emilio. Associated Press, 3 March 2020;
"The Extraordinary Decisions Facing Italian Doctors" by Yascha Mount. *The Atlantic*, 11 March 2020;
"Special Report: 'All is well'. In Italy, triage and lies for virus patients" by Emilio Parodi, Silvia Aloisi, & Pamela Barbaglia. Reuters, 16 March 2020; "Ethical Anguish in a Time of COVID-19" by Joel Shurkin. Inside Science, 27 March 2020.

had already shrunk my social life; all the canceled events simply made it smaller. The only other noticeable effect was a mammogram appointment, postponed until June. (The combination of my family history plus previous cancer scares keeps me diligent on screenings.) So I mustered my unfoggiest brain and added multiple reminders to my calendar.

As spring kicked up, I experienced my first intense spring allergies since childhood. Atlanta (unceded ancestral lands of the Creek, Muscogee, and Cherokee) is well-known for absurdly high pollen counts.[4] For the first time since middle school, I had pollen-induced, intense flu-like symptoms: sinus pressure, even higher fever, bodyache, and so on. Breathing outside made my sinuses burn.

By that point, for months I'd lived wanting to be still. Do nothing, all the time. Be still, be quiet. In stark contrast to how I'd always lived prior, as an artist and performer who didn't make a living from art and performance—by choice—I was always moving. Work, performances, music tours, volunteer work, a busy social life, years of consistent movement and contemplative practices. I was always moving, always in the flow of life, and I loved it. I found joy in everything.

In my current lethargy, I reminded mySelf to connect to some movement, somewhere. Asana and pranayama practice, short walks. Anything that got me out of my zombielike existence, in my cement body with cobweb lungs. Waterfalls tumbling. Still moving.

---

4   A "mellow" bad day is 1500. IYKYK.

All the while, I was struggling to navigate what was eventually called brain fog. I lived in a vaporous fuzz. Decisions required a lot of effort, which meant they required a lot of time. Even simple decisions: what to eat for breakfast, what socks to wear. Thoughts were made of mist.

At first, I attributed brain fog to lack of sleep. Since I had migraines or near-migraines every day, I figured I was just sleep-deprived. But the brain fog was more than a sleepy delay in collecting my thoughts.

For months, I'd go into the bathroom and immediately be confused when I crossed the threshold. First, I had the unsettling experience of seeing my reflection in the mirror. That person was me, but I didn't recognize her. I knew, intellectually, it was the same face, the same hair, the same body. But the familiar was a stranger. Someone I didn't know. Someone I'd never known.

I quickly conditioned myself to avert my eyes immediately from the mirror. Then, as I wiped my tears, the questions began.

Why did I come in here?
I mean, there are only three reasons to be here ... the
sink, the shower, the toilet.
... Which is it?
How long since I was last here?
...
Do I need to brush my teeth?
Maybe I smell and it's time to shower. Do I smell?

I skipped showering yesterday....
Also I'm too tired to shower.
...
Yeah, I'm tired every day. I'm fucking tired.
...
I should brush my teeth.
No, I should at least wash my face.
Or try to pee. Fuck, I feel like an infant being potty-trained ...
OK, this is ridiculous. I give up. I'll come back later.

Sometimes the closed door was to have privacy to cry.

Then I would give up trying to remember why I'd gone in there in the first place, and I would come back later, and the monologue would repeat itself, like a fugue. Wednesday at 2:57am, when I assiduously looked away from the mirror, again at 9:25am, when I closed my eyes while I pondered the same questions, again at 4:44pm, when I cast my eyes downward as I questioned myself. I wanted to be still. Just sit on the toilet seat, close my eyes, and disappear.

All over again on Monday at 2:34am and 9:17am and 7:24pm and 10:02pm. By then, I'd learned to look anywhere but the mirror. The floor, ceiling, corners, behind my eyelids—anything to avoid the mirror.

Again the next day. And the next. Saturday at 3:14am and 5:15am and 6:03am and 7:05am and and and ...

A similar fugue happened at my bookshelf. Tears and questions.

Yes, time to read. So ready for this.

Wait, what did I want to read?

Well, I have a stack of unread books ...

Poetry? That's a good idea, something less dense.

... Yeah, but maybe too abstract and metaphorical.

That's too much labor for my brain.

I need something less taxing.

... Or maybe I want a reread. Something I know, that won't be too much new information.

Soooo, a novel? Nonfiction ...

Hard to decide ... Something cheerful will make me feel worse.

Something depressing will make me feel worse.

I don't know if I can handle that.

I can't handle anything; who am I kidding ...

Never mind, I'll return to the chair.

Bookshelf crying was much more furtive, out of necessity, because my partner might walk by and see me. Ideal timing was when he was in a meeting, when he closed the door to his office. In those moments, I indulged my tears and felt like a spoiled, weak brat.

I wanted to be still. Just close my eyes, disappear into the pages. Become imaginary.

At 8:12am and 10:11am and 2:19pm and 4:15pm and and and and –

At least there were no mirrors near the bookshelf.

I lived in the same set of clothes for a few days at a time, until I put them in the laundry. That set of clothes went from bed to chair to meditation cushion to chair to asana mat to bed to chair. I wore the pandemic uniform of sweats and t-shirts to sleep (occasionally), eat, sit around, stare into space. Or old leggings and ratty sweatshirts, plus a long housecoat in the fall and winter (because I'm always cold) to doze, wander confusedly to the bathroom, stare blankly at the bookshelf.

My favorite clothing texture is super worn in t-shirts, followed closely by anything else with similar fabric. The smoothness and drape are so soothing. That one small choice at least brought a measure of comfort.

So much comfort, in fact, that I didn't change clothes very often. Less thinking, less effort. Usuallyn I changed clothes after two or three days, preferably before I detected any offensive odors. Didn't always happen, though, because there might only be a single shower in the span of wearing the same clothes for days. I already felt listless and gross from exhaustion, so I hated another reason to find myself disgusting.

Still moving, though less so still bathing.

I didn't shower in my clothes—though I have done that many times, other stories for other occasions—but only because dealing with a set of wet clothes would be more laborious than showering normally.

I never asked for help in undressing before or dressing after a shower. The thought of being so weak disgusted me as much as all the other things that disgusted me. Brain fog. Sleep deprivation. Exhaustion. Lack of basic care—by then my partner made nearly all our food and did most of the grocery shopping. I appreciated how much he did and I hated how much he did, with zero reciprocity from me.

And so, I clutched at this miniscule shred of control, never realizing it was more like a glass shard that cut deeply into me and bled me further. Now, I wish I'd asked for more help. Maybe that disgust with myself wouldn't have lasted so long. Maybe I would have had ephemeral moments of peace.

Or maybe I would have hated myself further.

Another thing I hated was the change in my meditation practice. Despite the skepticism of that meditation teacher on the retreat, I generally didn't find meditation taxing. Not that it's easy, of course. For the most part, though, I'd practiced meditation long enough that I didn't fight my resistance or my struggles.

Brain fog, however, destroyed my ability to concentrate. I could no longer sit and calmly focus. I used to surrender, gently, into less thinking. But my mind couldn't handle the practice. The closest I came to meditation was a sort of dissociative fog while sitting somewhere. Maybe near my bookshelf, as my thoughts trailed off. Or within sight of the bathroom, as I pondered whether I needed it.

From the outside, maybe I looked like I was meditating. But I was nowhere near, and if I'd had the energy I would have been angrier and more bitter.

Life was annoying. More than that, though, life was unnerving. And it never stopped. I soon became frustrated, then despondent at my inability to hold thought, take care of myself, or maintain any sort of schedule.

A typical job was impossible. Like many long-haulers, I was incapable of showing up to standard work hours. In the two years before I became sick, I worked mostly for charity, as an unpaid volunteer. It was far from financially ideal for my household, but I had been confident—like I had been for the life refresh in 2019 for my wide open future—that I'd transition into paying work by 2020. When I fell ill and was unable to work, nothing changed for us financially, because there was no income to lose. We were already calibrated to my lack of income.

My only work was on my own schedule: I taught a few classes online; I worked with people individually; I accepted contract jobs. They were possible because I needed only to be lucid and presentable for short spurts. No more than a couple hours at a time. But often just one, or even thirty minutes.

Working from home allowed my partner to be supportive in ways that were previously unavailable. By late spring, he had assumed the care of most of our household. After more than twenty years of cooking nearly all my own meals, I simply stopped. The mere thought of prepping ingredients exhausted me; I gave up without even thinking. I ate when he cooked me food. He stocked the kitchen and did most of the grocery shopping. When I went to the grocery, I got whatever was on his list.

Understandably, he was alarmed at my health. He constantly checked on me, which I both appreciated and resented. I barely answered his questions. Monosyllables. Impassive shrugs. I knew I was hurting him. Also that he knew I was lying. And that I knew he knew. My exhausted, defeated heart, though, didn't care enough to stop.

Sometimes, I leaned back in a chair with my eyes closed and told him I was too tired to talk. Which was, at least, true. I was still barely sleeping. Pain or coughing or both meant I often got up in the middle of the night. I attempted to read as much as possible. But reading was taxing on my brain, so more often I streamed shows or movies.

Other mornings I woke so early that I simply got up. Starting my day at 3:44am or 2:46am or 4:12am became common. Sometimes I dozed in the afternoons, sometimes not. Migraine pain sometimes makes sleep inevitable: my body is simply so exhausted that it has to rest. Migraine pain sometimes makes sleep impossible: the air hurts, which means it's impossible to rest my head on a pillow or even lean back in a chair without wanting to scream.

If you didn't already know that depression is a comorbidity in many illnesses—it's no surprise, if your life resembles any of this. Sleep deprivation gets depressing, over time. Over time, chronic pain and fatigue get depressing. Losing the self you recognize and the identity you know is depressing. Especially when there's no expectation, let alone certainty, of recovery.

As much as possible, I actively avoided the temptation of hope. Occasionally, I allowed a fantasy of anything but living in what amounted to an incessant migraine. I was certain, in those fanciful moments, of how good, how amazing I'd feel if I ever stopped being sick.

If you remember living through the shutdown—or years from now, when people who are too young to remember— you know the many facets of struggle everyone faced. The ever-rising death toll. Intense election campaigns. Renewed activations for civil rights. Escalating conspiracy theories. Given all of that, I hid my overwhelming experience, which I was sure no one could understand.

I took every opportunity for crying breaks. Crying about myself, crying about the world. Not just in the bathroom or in front of the bookshelf. The short walk from the grocery was always a good opportunity. On the way home, after I'd encountered people in the store and once I was past the only busy intersection, I allowed myself, behind my sunglasses, two minutes of crying, with the final two minutes to compose myself before reaching home.

Had I lived alone—though of course that was impossible—maybe I would have cried enough. I felt like I could cry forever, that there could never be enough opportunities to shed all the tears. I craved the catharsis of crying, embraced being the weeping woman, but I was afraid that would mean that I'd never stop. Or that I'd feel so hopeless I'd give up and make other plans.

I guarded my tears so closely that my partner, who lived in the same home, was the only person who witnessed or knew many significant details. And yet, I didn't tell him anything more than what he already saw. The world was suffering, and I didn't want him to suffer on my account. I worried that my experience was contagious, and I didn't want to poison him with my pain.

I already felt like a tremendous burden, and I didn't want to burden more people. Not to mention that many, many people were going through struggles of their own, whether Covid itself or Covid-adjacent issues such as unemployment, housing struggles, and school disruptions.

All my life I'd been a strong person. Hyper-independent. The person others call in a crisis, the person who figures out impossible situations, the person everyone seeks for advice. I have always believed that we all need to take care of each other. But I also wanted what I can admit, now, is impossible: *I* didn't want to need help. I wanted to be invulnerable, because I was afraid of being dismissed. I was afraid of being told that the real problem was that I wasn't strong enough.

I knew many friends would want to understand, would also be sympathetic to what I didn't even understand yet. Nonetheless, I didn't want their reactions. I didn't want people worrying or panicking on my behalf. More than anything, though, I was sure that I was too much. Too intense. Too depressing. Too exhausting, in those overwhelming times. Sure to be an unwelcome, unwanted burden.

By that time, I had deconditioned a lot of my shame and lack of self-trust. But the personal and collective intensity of Covid unwound a lot of those inner shifts, and I regressed to a lot of toxic patterns.

So I said nothing, and no one knew the whole truth. And I remained isolated, unwilling to be a fool or a burden or a fright or a buzzkill.

Moreover, plenty of people were quite vocal that they didn't care to understand, or even acknowledge. It's another layer to this experience, which I rarely see acknowledged: the damage to relationships with people who have been dismissive about Covid. In various ways: that the disease isn't real, or that it might be real, but exaggerated. That commentary was and still is extremely triggering. Those scripts match almost verbatim with what I was told from a young age: that I'm being melodramatic, that I don't really know what's happening, that I've invented what I'm "feeling."

But plenty of non-deniers were still dismissive. They didn't doubt the reality of Covid, but they also insisted it could be avoided with vitamins and high vibes. I encountered that perspective constantly in the first pandemic year. I lost count of social media posts about supplements and positive thinking. And I had people tell me directly, in real time, that they wouldn't get Covid because they were so high vibe.

Duuuuuude, you're one of the worthy ones! You tapped into that foolproof guarantee of not getting sick?! Because illness is for losers who don't know any better. That foolproof guarantee works for cancer too, right?

To be clear: "I won't get Covid/cancer/autoimmune illness because I'm so high vibe" is super gross spiritual bypassing. If you're around people saying these sorts of things, please find better people. If you're saying these sorts of things—for fuck's SAKE, shut up. Listen, learn, do better.

I often wondered—I still do—whether people would have spoken differently if I'd disclosed anything about my experience. But so many people were clear that they didn't want to understand, and at the time I was skeptical whether certain friendships could or would ever recover. And now, people who believe that my reality should be consigned to a collective past—a collective, amnesiac un-recollection— surely would say these same things to me now.

Consequently, I retreated from social media, to avoid all this garbage. Because those moments were ...

Difficult.

I don't want to be resentful, but that task is ...

Also difficult.

I want to transcend the past, but as someone with extremely limited energy, I can admit the task is constantly subordinated by other things I wish to do.

I felt like a wraith, a person made of smoke. At most, an observer of life. Not a participant. Social media exacerbated the feeling, which was another reason to avoid it. The wraith feeling was an imposter syndrome of sorts. It wasn't about being a "successful" or certain kind of human, but about whether I was human at all, in the ways I witnessed other people being human.

In spring, hummingbirds started visiting my yarden— drawn, indubitably, by the meadowscape of unkempt herbs and pollinators. I gazed at them for what seemed like hours at a time, in their whizzy journeys among the flowers. I realized, through the fog, that those unpredictable-to-me flight patterns reminded me of my own mind.

I continued dragging myself to the mat and to the cushion, whether at 8:37am or 12:14pm. I knew that my physical health depended on still moving. Before Covid, I could do vigorous cardio activities for hours at a time. Touching my toes was easy, even if I'd just gotten out of bed while camping in cold weather. A couple dozen pushups in a minute didn't require a giant effort.

With Covid, my body changed swiftly. I struggled to touch my toes. Even as the hacking cough decreased, I struggled to do any pushups. Mobility reduced. Muscles atrophied. Much of the day focused on recovery from my efforts to move, plus migraine management.

I needed that time to recover not just physically, but also emotionally and spiritually. Even in brief durations of practice, I was tired in both body and soul. I knew practice was essential for me. Concurrently, it brought immense mental and emotional anguish. Those times were raw. They helped my body, but also crystallized all the layers of pain. I had flashes of clarity, when I witnessed, fully, truly, how far gone I was. How exhausted I was, too exhausted to honor the anger and fear and sadness underneath it. I felt the fatigue more deeply, the pain and fevers more clearly, the despair more fully.

People often come to contemplative and embodiment practices because they feel better afterwards. That was certainly true for me when I came to yoga practices, nearly twenty years before I got Covid. Every time I left my mat or my meditation cushion, I felt better, or at least clearer.

But those same practices that had nourished me for years now brought me to the most intense anguish of my life.

Those contemplative and embodiment practices brought me
into the clearest experience of my pain. I was miserable every
time, the whole time. Every hacking break made me want to
quit. Just lie down and disappear. I was always glad to end
any practice session. But not because I felt better, in the sense
of improvement from before I started. I felt "better" because
I was done for the day.

And yet—still moving. Rainbows beaming and starlight
shimmering.

Even to me now, the *still moving* choice makes no sense.
Certainly it made no sense at the time. My egoic, insecure
mind constantly teased me with the rationale that there was
no point in doing difficult things that only brought me into
more despair.

Then again, I've never been one to worship logic above
all else. An optimistic way to explain it would be that somewhere inside was a tiny spark of hope. If I wanted to peddle
inspiration, I'd declare that emphatically, enthusiastically:

> ## "DEEP DOWN, I JUST *KNEW*
> ## I'D GET BETTER!
> ## I JUST HAD TO STAY POSITIVE."

I prefer honesty, though. What I recognized then and what
remains true now is that I didn't want to forfeit my well-being, even when I saw no path towards feeling better. I wasn't
hopeful, but I knew that giving up on my daily practice
would then justify completely self-destructive behaviors.

Again, if I wanted to peddle shiny, bypassing optimism:

> "I JUST *KNEW* THAT **ONE DAY** I'D OVERCOME
> THIS ILLNESS!
> YOU JUST HAVE TO KEEP THE FAITH.
> DON'T. GIVE. UP!"

But I still prefer honesty, and the truth is that I was scared of what a forfeit would unleash. If I spurned my own delicate lifeline of breathwork, meditation, and time on my mat, I was confident that I'd slide quickly into even worse lethargy. Nothing would stop me from completely disengaging from the world. I know how to plan. I could easily slide into loads of alcohol, plenty of cannabis. Maybe source some sleeping pills or other painkillers.

I mean, if I give up, why not give up completely, right? No reason to attempt a sleep schedule. No reason not to numb the pain as utterly as possible, to consume whatever substances make it disappear. I could make the pain disappear, and in the process I could disappear.

I saw that possibility, clearly. So I chose pain I already knew, out of fear of destruction. And I don't regret choosing from fear. Hope, optimism, faith were all unavailable. I'm not here to peddle fabricated inspiration.

Not that anyone knew, at the time, about any of this. I was too tired, too scared, too overwhelmed by illness and lockdown and fires and elections and conspiracies. Body bags delivered to a reservation, instead of the supplies that the

Indigenous population requested.[5] The world losing its mind.

By late spring, I thought I was losing my mind, after months of questioning it. I considered tracking my symptoms, making a log. I researched early onset dementia. I wondered whether I'd continue to live in my body for a few more decades, but my mind would depart much sooner. Maybe the departure had already begun and would simply continue, for the rest of my life.

It was terrifying to consider, but also reasonable. Dementia and Alzheimer's run in both sides of my family.

In the early stages of dementia and Alzheimer's, one of the first areas of the brain affected is the hippocampus. The hippocampus is named for the Greek word for seahorse, due to the physical resemblance between the brain structure and the sea creature. Both hemispheres of the brain have one, and the purpose of the pair is to consolidate memories from short-term to long-term, as well as enable spatial memory. Among other things.

I already knew that memory can be slippery and unreliable. But not until Covid did I see it as so fragile. Not unlike seahorses, which are gentle, timid creatures that suffer from various threats, including overfishing, loss of habitat, and demand for souvenirs. Among other things.

During the incessant bullying of my teen years, I gazed at seahorses wistfully, wishing for their armored bodies.

---

5   "Native American health center asked for COVID-19 supplies. It got body bags instead." by Erik Ortiz. *NBC News*, 6 May 2020.

Years later, I wished my brain could have that armor.

My seahorse musings led me down an internet vortex, learning about a mythological hippocampus, an animal with the upper body of a horse and lower body of a fish. Then I really wished my brain could feel more like this powerful, agile, versatile hippocampus.

However, my brain felt more like real seahorses, animals which are not actually good swimmers. In their native environments, they are awkward and slow, curling their prehensile tails around something stationary, living at the mercy of currents and circumstances. My mind was constantly fluttering, like the tiny fins of a seahorse, seeking to grasp something safe and solid.

If anything, the virus felt like a tapeworm in my brain. Consuming thoughts before they even existed. A flat, ravenous, insatiable pest, devouring connections, burrowing itself into the folds of my mind.

For example: I happened to learn, when I was updating some bank accounts, that I'd forgotten my Social Security number, which I'd memorized as a teenager.[6] The form asked for the final four digits as verification, and I couldn't remember. I thought about the beginning numbers, that they might spark my memory for the final four. But I couldn't remem-

---

6   If you're not familiar with Social Security Numbers, they are issued
     to US citizens, permanent residents, and other individuals. One's
     SSN is used for loads of applications—schools, residences, loans,
     bank accounts—over the years. I used to know my SSN more readily
     than my mobile phone number.

ber the start. Then I went through all the digits, noticing if any felt familiar as the beginning or the end of my SSN. Nothing. And there are only ten digits to try. I had to dig through personal documents to find it.

Mid-year, I learned about Long Covid.[7] That people were having difficult experiences like mine and also much worse, with no correlation to the severity of their acute illness.

For the first time, I realized I might not be losing my mind, in that I wasn't imagining things. But also that I might actually be losing my mind, in that this squirrelly, tapewormy illness burrows into the brain. And the extent to which is still unknown.

And somehow, I was still moving. Tides writhing. Trees breathing.

I don't know if you've made bargains with the universe, or with whatever/whomever you might believe in. Luck and privilege got me well into adulthood before the huge bargains appeared. Long Covid was the first time I tried to broker big deals. Any of my cosmic bargains from before, in comparison—hoping to be hired for a job or having a romantic interest call me back—revealed themselves as much lower stakes than they seemed at the time.

If I heal from this, I'll never stray from my purpose.

---

7   "COVID-19 can last for several months" by Ed Yong. *The Atlantic*, 4 June 2020; "Long-haulers are redefining COVID-19" by Ed Yong. *The Atlantic*, 19 August 2020.

I'll never stray from my purpose!
... Not that I know what my purpose is.
But if I get better, I will dedicate all my energy to
figuring it out and never losing sight of it.
If I can think again, if I can breathe again, I will be
steadfast and clear and perfect.
Just let me know what that means, and I'll do it all, I
swear.

Not much of a bargaining chip with the universe, but at least I was honest about my desperation. I'd quit my old life; since then I'd been incapable of making anything new to offer in exchange.

Bargains. Proof. Still moving. Fireflies flashing, moths fluttering, crickets chirping, cicadas buzzing.

Meanwhile, the world was on fire. In some places very literally, in historic wildfires. Whereas other metaphorical fires, some hundreds of years old, were intensifying. Watching the protests against police brutality was inspiring. I was relieved at the willingness to confront racism more deeply, hoping that it would grow into a larger shift.

At any other time prior in my life, I would have joined the protests. But I knew I didn't have the energy. I also had that postponed mammogram, in the middle of June. The test had a certain urgency for me, and I didn't want to postpone again.

But without rescheduling, I was reluctant to participate. Given the level of exposure at protests, I didn't want to subject myself or healthcare workers—where I live, where I go, most of the ones I encounter are Black women—to the risk of contagion.

So, I didn't join the protests, which was disappointing. After the dull grey vibrations of the machine, I did receive clean results from the mammogram, which was heartening.

Not long after the surge of protests, I found a plastic baggie of dog shit in front of my home. More specifically, on the middle of the sidewalk, right by the Black Lives Matter sign in my yard. It was one of those moments when I wanted to say, "This is some bullshit." Except that this was actual dog shit.

Disappointing, and a bit puzzling. That spring and summer, more BLM signs appeared in the home windows and front yards of white residents nearby. Mine had been in my yard for years, without any bags of excrement dropped in front of it.

A few weeks after the dog shit day was my first pandemic birthday. Everyone had that milestone, eventually, and by the time it was my turn, enough time had elapsed to witness the many ways people managed living in a pandemic, or not. I was envious of anyone with a life, anyone not sick. I was especially envious of people with successful pandemic pivots.

The most obvious example was my friend Stella, a gifted healer in the midst of a huge life change. About a month after the shutdown began, she contracted Covid. I was grateful for her frequent updates, though they were scary: she had several days of temperatures over 100° F (38° C). A gifted healer, she never lost perspective on her larger purpose—she hoped to recover quickly and be even more resilient, so that she could continue her healing practice.

Soon after that, before I even understood the existence of Long Covid, she'd cashed out all her savings, bought a small lot in the mountains, and started building a cabin for one. And while she had plenty of privilege, she also didn't have a safety net. She was single, and her immediate family was dead or estranged.

I admired her bold choice, in a time of so much uncertainty. Always willing to live her own life, she had her own business and frequently went camping with only her dog for company. We always texted frequently, and pre-pandemic we spent a lot of time together. In the lockdown, phone calls replaced those in-person times. I had a standing invitation to visit, but I was too tired, too despondent. Nothing to do with her personally—I wasn't fully present or available to anyone, including myself.

Not to mention that I knew I would find it discouraging. I was happy for her, yet also envious. She had an expanding, exciting life, whereas mine was stagnant, diminishing. Nevertheless, I cheered on her progress, while I endeavored to be still moving, in what felt like meaningless, miserable ways.

A few days after my midsummer birthday, she visited me. Given that I'm a summer baby, I didn't mind the swampy heat of the season. (Cold, in fact, is a migraine trigger for me.) I mustered the energy for both a shower and clean clothes. I pep talked my cement and cobwebs for a fun afternoon with a loved one.

We walked in that swampy heat to retrieve takeout from a nearby restaurant, and returned to my place to eat on the porch. Over tacos on house tortillas and maduros, we discussed her house construction, while our sweat nominally dried, or at least abated, to the light sheen of a humid, hot afternoon. Understandably, she was nervous about putting all of her savings into the project. I reminded her that she was capable, and that I enjoyed seeing all the updates.

That was true; I did. But—hopefully understandably—those updates were also hard for me. Her life was dynamic. For months, I'd been watching her actively chart her life and create her future. Those moments made me viscerally aware of my reality, different in every meaningful way.

Her life was so, so good. After some rough years, she was in a lot of joy. And despite my twinges of envy, I was happy to see her claiming her life the way she wanted. I was certain that sharing my pain would kill her joy.

And so, I shared as little as possible about myself. Nothing faithful to the actual intensity and scope of my experience. Nothing truly accurate. Just that I had more headaches than usual; I was tired most of the time.

All of my friends and loved ones know about my chronic illness, but almost none have witnessed me with migraines. The only exceptions: my partner and Stella. They're the only people who knew and who had been with me while migraines were happening. I didn't lie by falsehood. But I definitely lied by omission.

And if I weren't fully honest with the two people who'd been with me at my worst, I was definitely not fully honest with anyone else. I followed the same limited script with everyone: I had a lot of migraines and I was tired. This continued for years, at coffee dates, lunch, walks outside, video calls.

I never deviated with anyone, including my closest friends. Especially them. Including my brother, who's been my most enthusiastic supporter longer than anyone else. He and others knew I was struggling, but nowhere close to the actual extent. The world was on fire; the world was depressing; I didn't want to poison my loved ones with my pain.

These days, many people are familiar with neurodivergence masking. But masking also happens with chronic illness. It includes wan smiles in a depressive episode or a cheery demeanor with back pain. But it's often more than that. Often it's directing all available energy—all of the precious, tiny amount of energy that even exists—towards concealing your experience.

Because explaining and answering questions drain more energy than masking. Because enduring well-intentioned sympathy that emerges from questions you don't want to consider—questions like "Are you going to be ok?" or "What can I do?"—is also more taxing than masking.

Those kinds of questions are challenging because the answers often make the questioners uncomfortable. "Are you

going to be ok?" — in regards to Long Covid, the answer
was *Not necessarily, I have no idea; there's no indication that this
will ever improve.*

And Stella was already familiar with my chronic illness.
Still, I didn't want to be a buzzkill to her joy. I didn't want
to burden her with worrying about me. That swampy summer afternoon on the porch, I was content to hear about the
excitement and expansion in her life, with no mention of
my own struggles.

And so, with one of my dearest friends, I said nothing.
More nothing in my life.

After she left, I rested for the remainder of the day and
into the next, after the physical exertion and the energetic
labor. All of which I was glad to expend, but I had to go far
beyond my capacity.

As dissolved time continued, I dragged myself to practice. Every day, I wanted to stay in bed. Lie there and be
still. Indefinitely. Fervently, futilely, I wanted the stillness
to end the pain. I wanted to sleep forever and dream about
delightful alternate realities to my current one.

However, my physical pain was such that I couldn't stay
in bed. My body, especially my neck and shoulders, hurt
too much to stay horizontal. Despite my desire to sleep
indefinitely, lying in bed (or anywhere) hurt enough for
me to sit upright, and shuffle to my foggy cement wraith
nothing life, to the repeated confusions in the bathroom or
at the bookshelf. To the concerned looks of my partner, to
whom I answered questions in mumbles and monosyllables.

I'd stopped hacking cobwebs by then, but I barely noticed.

In September, I got a high fever, seemingly out of nowhere, in my nothingzone life. At any other time, this would not have been notable. But it was my first high fever in almost a year.

I woke up in the middle of the night, exploded out of bed. And had a panic attack.

Gladly willing to disregard the usual migraine trigger of cold, I chugged multiple glasses of ice water. (I constantly run cold; I only drink ice water in the worst instances of heat or dehydration.) I laid naked on the sofa on my porch, rubbing a washcloth, which I'd dunked in ice water, all over my skin. Anything to lower the temperature.[8]

I was terrified of backsliding. Through the screaming and crying, I begged not to be acutely ill again.

The next morning—still moving. I sat on my cushion, rolled out my mat, as always.

I had one truly delightful, joyous day in 2020. On the afternoon of November 7th, my partner and I started hearing incessant car horns. We assumed, at first, that there was an accident or especially bad traffic. After about twenty minutes, we realized the noise was celebration at the election results that had just been called. A new president had been elected.

I leaned into all my reserves, and we walked to a

---

8   Disclaimer: This is not informed medical advice. Obvs.

nearby park, where hundreds of elated people celebrated with costumes, horns, drums, and signs. Many drivers honked their horns, including those in city buses and garbage trucks.

I'm often overwhelmed by crowds, but this was a rare occasion that I wanted to dance and scream and frolic. On this day, I mostly sat and observed. When I closed my eyes, I could see colors and textures from all the horns and drums and cheers. And even though I was too tired to join in, I was so relieved and grateful that I didn't care about the noise or my fatigue.

In eight years of living in that area, that afternoon is in my top five best days. I was extra exhausted for the next week, but I didn't mind.

By that late in the year, I'd been sick long enough to notice patterns. In addition to sleep deprivation, another complicating factor was my menstrual cycle, which is a common migraine trigger. After decades of predictable duration and bleeding patterns, my cycle had gone haywire: inconsistent bleeding, inconsistent duration. I formerly had the ability to predict, with high accuracy, the days I needed more rest, the days more likely to trigger headaches. But by 2020, that consistency was gone. Certainly, the inconsistency was in a closed loop with sleep deprivation and pain and everything else.

I don't hate my body, and I don't see my menstrual cycle as dirty or obscene. In fact, it's the opposite; I consider my cycle sacred and holy. For most of the decades I've been bleeding, I charted my cycle, a process that yields plenty of insights.[9]

The shifts were notable. For example, I had constant fevers in late 2019 and all of 2020. I know my usual, healthy temperature range because part of my charting was taking my temperature every morning. Those numbers don't lie. Month after month, cycle after cycle, my body temperatures were consistently elevated, with exceptions only a couple days a month at most.

In other words, I was running a fever nearly every day of 2020. Looking at charts before and after that year, I had hundreds of days of elevated temperatures.

Which certainly aggravates migraines and brain fog and sleep deprivation and pain and everything else.

Nothing is particularly pleasant, in my experience, with a fever. Not reading, not taking walks. Definitely not pranayama or not asana practice. Not even sitting in a chair staring into space. Sounds exaggerate when I have a fever. My hand sliding along a sheet is as loud as thunder overhead during a storm. A sigh reverberates like a giant fan. Which means actual loud noises are incredibly painful.

You know that song about the guy who works in the but-

---

9   Nowadays, that kind of charting could be incriminating, should I have certain health concerns. I want to be clear that my menstrual charting before *Dobbs v. Jackson Women's Health Organization* is not necessarily reflective of menstrual charting (if any) after *Dobbs v. Jackson Women's Health Organization*. If we lived in a world that honored body autonomy, I would share more. But as we don't, I'm sure you understand my need for privacy.

ton factory? I learned it as "Hi, my name is Joe / I got a wife and 3 kids / and I work in a button factory." Each verse of this (heteronormative, capitalist) song has Joe's boss telling him to turn a button with a certain body part. By the end of the song, Joe's right hand, left hand, right foot, left foot, shoulders, head, eyes, and anything else the songleader can imagine are all wildly moving, to show how overwhelmed Joe is at his job.

I felt like I was the end of the song, all the time. Except not just my limbs, but also my internal organs, my nervous system, blood vessels, and anything else that could twist itself around. My pancreas, my vagus nerve, my plantar fascia, my whole body flailing and writhing and thrashing.

That was my life of disrupted sleep and migraines and crying and disordered appetite and migraines and brain fog and crying and despair and disrupted sleep and pain. And pain. Pain.

Pain. Always pain.

At that point, I told myself to re-evaluate my future. To reconsider what I thought was possible. That wide open future I had been so confident to create was an illusion. Maybe I would never fully recover. Maybe my actual future was this empty shell of a life.

Not knowing how permanent or temporary Long Covid would be was the only thing worse than living with it.

I had been telling myself to have hope for feeling better. But perhaps that was foolish. Maybe I didn't have the start of dementia or Alzheimer's, but I'd lived through nearly four hundred days of steady fevers. Instead of hope, perhaps I needed to consider more realistic scenarios. Options grounded in recent experience pointed me to considering that I might never work again, or make art again, or exist in ways I had before. That expecting to return to anything resembling my previous normalcy was unlikely, if not impossible.

I kept moving, but I slowed. I resigned myself to aiming for acceptance of an unwanted life and an unwanted future.

One of the reasons I was still moving, despite all of this, is because I've lived with chronic pain from such a young age. In fact, one of the easiest ways to describe me is that I've always had a high pain tolerance. It's an easy description because of the best and worst things about it.

The best thing about a high pain tolerance: You can endure a lot of pain.

The worst thing about a high pain tolerance: You can endure a lot of pain.

Meaning that in the best of times, you are not derailed by bad things: bad luck, bad circumstances, or bad people. But in the worst of times, you can be far too generous and accommodating of bad things, especially bad circumstances and bad people.

I've always had a high tolerance for pain. Long Covid, though, was hitting the furthest edges of that tolerance, more than I'd ever confronted.

By now, you might be thinking that this is all a terrible way to live. I agree.

I didn't want to live. Not if living meant that this was my baseline existence.

Ideation—about living, about inflicting additional pain on myself—was a balm.[10] Distraction, fantasies, daydreams from the relentless, debilitating pain, fear, overwhelm, despair.

As someone who's lived with a chronic illness for over thirty years, I well know the power of the imagination to inspire and soothe. For many people with chronic conditions, ideation is not an unusual coping mechanism. It's escapism, imagining a (kind of) existence in which the unbearable pain is gone. Perhaps more accurately, a departure, a disconnection from chronic pain. Ideation has always provided solace for me.

So much of the pain from chronic illness is embedded in the body. When your body constantly holds extreme pain, it's difficult not to despise what you can't escape. It's very easy to disengage.

Possibilities of not being in the body—even possibilities that could be deemed violent—create a blissful (and temporary) alternative reality of leaving the body.

That kind of ideation, for me, is a flight of fancy. I know that "flight of fancy" makes many people think of butterfly nets and picnics. But for me, ideation provides the same peaceful reprieve.

Not to mention that pain and harm are siren songs in many contexts. Violent excitement, or sexual thrill.

For me, something else entirely.

Knives are my siren song. Especially those with a sub-

---

10   To be clear, since there are many types of ideation: in this work, ideation refers specifically to self-harm and suicidal thoughts.

tle slope to the blade, though I also appreciate the artistry of a sharp crescent. I have some translucent silk as fine and soft as delicate oil. Yet when folded, it has the heft of a knife. I imagine a blade like this fabric, so fine that its cuts feel like whispers of silk.

I imagine this silky, oily blade separating layers of my skin. Cuts so fine so as not to cause any pain at the moment of impact, yet deep enough to create pools of blood, that seep and wind their way like water on a landscape.

So peaceful, this flight of fancy.

Fun fact: I pass out at the sight of (non-menstrual) blood. From anyone, including me. I once cut my hand at work, and even though the cut was not serious, requiring nothing beyond basic first aid, I was immediately nauseous and light-headed. A coworker helped me stagger to the bathroom, where she left me standing with my hand under running water. When she returned with supplies two minutes later, she found me face-up on the cold floor: unconscious, blood pooling in my palm and onto the floor. Water still running.

That's how the silky blade and the fine cuts are flights of fancy—I would struggle mightily to live them out.

For me, ideation of self-harm brings me into a fantasy that's removed enough from reality to be engaging, yet not so far that I dismiss it as unbelievable fiction. I distract myself from the actual pain in my body, to not-real, but still believable, pain.

The absence of pain is too ridiculous of a fiction for me to entertain.

Out in the world, though, the prevailing attitude I encounter about ideation is that it is always a red flag, that it is absolutely a sign of imminent danger. I've encountered this perspective from nearly all people without chronic illness, including trained professionals in healthcare.

To be clear: this is not to say that ideation is not a big deal. Far from it. I am glad that ideation is taken seriously. It can be a sign of danger, of someone's potential to harm or already existent harm.[11]

As someone with a chronic illness, I think this perspective lacks nuance. I was taught to believe that ideation always-must-definitely-absolutely is a Bad Thing, that it always-must-definitely-absolutely will lead to suicide. Now that I've had decades of managing chronic illness and eventually Long Covid, I think ideation is reasonable and often inevitable. Ideation belongs in context; it does not mean the same thing, or have the same implications, for all people. Ideation is a spectrum, not an on/off switch.

That doesn't mean not to care. We need to care, deeply. For me, though, the issue is not if ideation exists. The issue is how to support people living with it. People who have ideation need care. But suicide counseling might not be the biggest help for some of them. Things like access to health-

---

11   If this is you—if you're making plans that can't be changed—please seek support. Please. In the US, you can call 988. 988lifeline. org has specific resources for Black mental health, indigenous populations, veterans, LGBTQIA+, attempt survivors, loss survivors, neurodivergents, Covid, en español, and more.

care, affordable housing, food security, and disability services might make a much bigger difference.

When the world refuses to acknowledge the range within ideation, it becomes stigmatized and people become even more isolated. Years ago, when I was single and lived alone, I was too terrified to admit to any ideation. I was afraid of its impact on my relationships. I was afraid of being seen as incompetent at my job. I was afraid of being forced into treatment I did not want.

That silence also meant that I had no support. Likewise, with Long Covid, this is exactly why I didn't seek medical attention. I was afraid of being dismissed or invalidated. But the opposite extreme is worse. I have witnessed too many examples of people being medicated or even institutionalized against their will, to trust that someone wouldn't become so fixated, with a panicked or shrill reaction, that I wouldn't receive the support I truly needed.

Any intense experience creates a reckoning: acute or chronic, predicted or unexpected. When pain, despair, rage, and the like are ongoing and no longer surprising, ideation is reasonable, if not inevitable.

Many people can't handle that truth. Moreover, plenty of people live their entire lives with nary a soul ever being fully, true-ly honest with them.

For example, I could never count the times I have heard or read "Just remember life always turns out for the best." Or that it takes both rain and sunshine to make a rainbow. Or that sad thoughts are like clouds, that eventually will pass.

Or that if I'm struggling, what would REALLY HELP SERIOUSLY SO MUCH is a gratitude journal.

Equally harmful are people who profess that they can support healing, but don't truly have the capacity. I've encountered enough people who've said they want me to be honest, but the moment I start, I'm told not to call in bad energy, that I'm manifesting my own illness with my negative mindset, and that I need to take a deep breath and see that it's all one, man.

Well-meaning, caring folks say these things, or post memes with them. As though a heavily filtered photo of yellow roses with "*Practice gratitude*" in bridesmaid font somehow makes the sentiment more effective.

It doesn't. Not for me.

I recognize that people share these things with good intentions. That advice is nice for people having a tough day. Or a rough week. I have to believe that people saying and sharing these things don't understand that for some of us, the view doesn't change.

Those "clouds" are in fact the sky.

I also recognize that when people don't know what to say, they frequently default to optimism. Or they don't want to admit they're afraid, so they default to optimism. If you've done this—like I have, before I better understood illness, depression, trauma, and other struggles—please know that it can land as dismissal. Or as a lack of concern, which I imagine is the opposite of what you want.

If you only take one thing from reading this extended

missive, let it not be anecdotes or new perspectives about Long Covid. Let it be to know that so many people suffer alone, because others are unable to witness their experience, and instead fixate on fate or gratitude or optimism. I wanted to avoid those responses entirely, which is partly why I didn't share about my experience for such a long time.

Sharing struggles and "negative" emotions often makes you feel like a burden—I think most people have felt that. And who wants to be a burden? The reluctance to feel like a burden fuels fears of losing friendships, fears of being treated badly by doctors, even fear of institutionalization. So, with that knowledge, please consider more nuance about ideation.

What that meant for me —

I begged for death.

I want to be done. Please make it be over.

I begged for death.

I'm done. I'm complete. I want to be gone.

I begged for death by the day, by the hour, eventually by the breath. I begged for death.

Please. Please soon. People will understand.

I was still moving, and I begged for death.

All my aspirations no longer seemed possible. I was convinced that I didn't have a future—certainly not a future I wanted. I didn't have a present that I wanted. I was nowhere near dying—I was never hospitalized, never had emergencies. But I was so far from living. If I had to fight to breathe and hurt to think, to fight to think and hurt to breathe—I wanted out. I wanted to turn in my notice, like quitting a job.

I am the weeping woman. I dwell in the vale of tears. I am the vale of all the tears.

I told the universe that I was at peace. I was unattached to those now-impossible hopes. I begged for death.

I want to be done. Now.

Please make it be over.

Done, please. Please, done.

I want to be gone.

I'm done. I'm complete.

Soon. Gone. Soon.

Today is fine. Please be soon. I know my loved ones will understand. They support me.

I am the weeping woman. I dwell in the vale of tears. I am the vale of all the tears.

I am grief. I am shattered. I will never be whole.

I am gone.

In a year in which I felt encased in cotton balls, wax paper, gauze, and bubble wrap, one of the clearest truths was that I must be miserable company. Everyone everywhere was already struggling in their own ways. I didn't want to burden anyone with my despair.

One day, I encountered a void. Maybe it was The Void, depending on your cosmology. But once I tripped onto the edge, I let myself tumble into this abyss.

To be clear: it wasn't The Primordial Void, Brimming With Potentiality.

If I were of a certain religious bent, I might call it purgatory. But I'm not bent that way.

It was just a void. Void of everything. A void brimming with nothing. No textures, no sights, no sounds, no tastes, no smells. My synesthesia flattened. The dull sensory experience was not unlike my life in general, encased in gauze and bubble wrap.

No thoughts, no feelings. A seasonless nothingplace.

This void was beyond. Beyond anything I could have imagined.

More than that, though, this void was...gone. Nothingzone.

And yet it existed. It was a place, energetically.

As much as I had nothing to enjoy while being there, it tugged like a siren song. Though there was neither song nor siren.

So I would sit in a chair, sometimes all afternoon, and be in this void. I mean, I had nothing to do. No energy for a job, no energy for intimacy with my partner. Way too much shame to tell anyone how far gone I was.

I never felt happiness or joy in the void. At first, that seemed terrible. But once I observed carefully, I realized it wasn't. Because I didn't feel.

So I hung out in the void, day after day after day. I knew that I "should" have found it horrific. But I didn't.

It was the only place where my current reality didn't make me feel less, didn't make me feel guilty for constantly begging for death.

In this void, I had no shame for these pleas. I had no grief for aspirations I thought were now wasted.

But not because I felt better. But because there was nothing. Nothing to grieve, nothing to desire.

In this void, I was the same. Same body, same spirit. The difference from usual life was that being as I was didn't make anything bad or unpleasant. In this nothingland, everything collapsed. No good, no bad, not even neutral. Just nothing.

I had always thought of numbness as a lack of feeling when feeling should be present, or dulled feelings that are actually stronger. The void showed me a different numbness, of a lack of *existence* of feeling. In the void, emotions were mental constructs. But without substance, because they didn't exist.

I indulged in thought experiments, to test this numb nothing place. In addition to passing out at the sight of blood, I have a very strong gag reflex; the mere thought of something even mildly gross can invoke nausea. So, I imagined rot, stench, vomit—all things that would normally shock me into sensation.

Nothing.

I escalated to gruesome scenarios. Grisly accidents with mangled limbs. All-consuming diseases with disgusting physical symptoms.

Still, nothing.

Moreover, I didn't react to feeling nothing. No frustration or irritation at my indifference. I was beyond reaction, beyond care, beyond all judgement or attachment.

Then I considered my typical coping scenarios. I imagined the jackhammer in my shoulders. The meat tenderizer in my sinew. Blades like silk, slicing my skin. All flights of fancy I find soothing.

Still. Nothing.

Being in the dissociation of this void, I could hold space for the ending I craved. I could imagine being gone, because I already was, while in this void of nothing.

I told the universe that my loved ones would understand, that they didn't want me to live in this nothingland, nor the misery of "regular" life outside of it.

I begged for death.

I knew, intellectually, that my loved ones would be sad. That they would grieve. But I didn't care enough to not to beg. I felt nothing for their potential pain. Now, those recollections make me question my capacity for love. Do I truly love people if I'm willing to create that much pain for them? I, who knows so much about pain.

I thought only of a different existence, away from all the pain—pain that wouldn't exist if I weren't alive.

And if you ideate all of this, ideating plans can happen quite naturally.

Ideation is why I make very particular life choices. For example, I don't imbibe much alcohol. The few spirits in my house are much more likely to be used in homemade herbal remedies than in cocktails. Ideation is why I have never sought prescriptions, whether for pain or insomnia or anything else, despite a life of chronic pain and a Long Covid experience marked by insomnia. Why I don't have firearms in my home. Despite my appreciation for beautiful blades, why I don't have a collection. Ideation is why I've never tried heroin or any other opiates.

You're more likely to use something that's nearby, and these things, for me, are too destructive to allow them to be accessible. There is a difference between imagining and planning, but when options are readily available, that distance between imagination and plan shrinks.

I know how to plan. Planning is easy. So easy that I don't trust myself not to plan, if everything else is accessible. I know that I need to keep certain things distant, in order to prevent planning. To prevent making big decisions in the moments when I don't want to feel better.

My daily practice has always been the most powerful way to maintain that distance. Without it, the gap to the next steps are all too close and all too easy.

Another way I avoided sliding into these plans was to plan other steps. I drafted goodbye/apology letters to my loved ones. I managed many, many paragraphs for multiple people before I was disgusted and ashamed.

Who was this person, who cared so little for those who love her? The specter me, the smoky wraith. But in that moment, that disregard for my loved ones was absolutely real.

Once, the universe responded to my pleas. As often as possible, I rode my bicycle. Any distance was strenuous, so I didn't need to go far. Nor did I go fast; I coasted as much as possible, hoarding exertion for uphills. One beautiful day, as I savored the sun and breeze and the fleeting enjoyment of riding my bike slowly around my neighborhood, I repeated my common thought, my plea for an ending.

As I looked ahead to a green light, I wondered if the universe might ever answer. Perhaps it would choose an unexpected moment. As that thought registered, I watched a car in the opposite direction plow through the opposite red light.

I was within seconds of being in that intersection. Had I been a little faster, I would have been crushed.

Shaking, I stopped pedaling, allowing the bike to decelerate. I cruised, slowly, safely, through the intersection. My shaking didn't stop until well after returning home.

I see. I understand. I know. Thank you for making it clear.

Still moving. Comets hurtling.

I wanted to heed the communication. But I still frequently slipped into the void, where it didn't matter that I might not get better.

I dwell in the vale of tears. I am the vale of all the tears. In the world I am the weeping woman. But I don't need that here.

I am shattered. I will never be whole. I want to be still.

The collectively subdued holidays at the end of 2020 didn't register as any less intense than usual for me. By that time, I was more than a year into daily fevers, headaches, sleep deprivation, brain fog, depression. Body constantly tensed, shoulders and jaw always clenched. Crying behind sunglasses, wanting to disappear, begging the universe not to exist, if existence meant living like this.

My muscles had atrophied all year. I couldn't do a single

pushup; I couldn't touch my toes without straining. By the end of the year, I had gained more than twenty-five percent of my body weight.

The weight gain created a big increase in bra cup size, which I semi-affectionately but also despondently called my Covid cleavage. Semi-affectionately because I didn't (and don't) want to hate my body. But I didn't enjoy a larger bust. Covid cleavage tugged my already aggravated granite shoulders, which activated more migraines. Outside of the lockdown uniform of baggy sweats and t-shirts, my clothes didn't fit.

I was physically bigger, with the same invisible illness I'd had for decades. And with a new invisible illness that many people didn't know existed. And plenty of people, if they were told of its existence, would deny it anyway.

I didn't recognize myself; nothing was familiar. Different body, blasted mind, beaten spirit—a wraith life that didn't even feel real, with no idea whether the conditions were permanent. I avoided not just looking in mirrors, but at any reflective surfaces. I avoided being in photos.

Seeing a stranger in the mirror, for such a long time, was one of the most unsettling experiences of my life. And "I" was this stranger, a changeling of mySelf.

A few years before I contracted Covid, a dear friend gave me a toast at a party. By then, we'd known each other for twenty years. She said I was "joy embodied." She'd seen it from the moment we met, that it was the nature of my being.

Joy was often my default setting. Finding beauty everywhere: in flowers growing in sidewalk cracks, the colors at twilight, morning birdsong. Jumping in leaf piles. Making faces at babies and enjoying their delightful, magical laughter. Appreciating whimsical socks, silly t-shirts, mismatched sheets and towels. Singing in the shower. Being the first person on a dance floor. Sunset chasing, cloud watching, sky gazing.

I think if you asked people who know me, they'd say I was joyful despite migraines. That's true, but I've also been chronically ill for so long that I don't remember much of my life before migraines. I think it's equally true that I was joyful because of migraines—because chronic illness reminds you, repeatedly, that everything in life is ephemeral. Seek joy, seize joy, savor joy, scatter joy.

At that toast, no one disagreed, including me. After more than a year of Long Covid, though, I believed that person who embodied joy was dead. The tapeworm, bloated on my brain, had folded itself in every crevice, gorging on my thoughts, gobbling and devouring sparks of inspiration, and chomping on memories.

I had already deemed myself the weeping woman. I decided that my purpose was to be the person who was always grieving, always crying, questioning my sanity every day. I was the reminder of suffering. Aimlessly wandering, sporadically dozing, constantly begging, all while in excruciating pain. I had nothing for joy.

On January 1st, 2021, anyone old enough to understand 2020 was tuning into the collective determination to have a good year. At the end of 2020, I had no inclinations towards optimism. But even I savored the freshness of the new year. Just as I'd attended that meditation retreat in the hopes of a fresh start, I was ready for 2021 to be The Year™.

Really, though, my hopes were due to the sustained, far-reaching efforts of voting organizations and volunteers across the country. In my state, two Senate seats were up for election, both with challengers against incumbents. Campaigning and activism got going in summer 2020, and by September, I was receiving daily calls and texts. I would have been more annoyed if I didn't recognize the significance of the elections: those two seats would determine the party leadership of the Senate.

Concurrently with the texts and calls, my mailbox constantly received handwritten notes and postcards (in addition to the usual, official political mailers). I was amazed at people so dedicated that they volunteered to write—by hand, never typed—and mail personal cards with my name. Sometimes the writers added drawings or stickers. I saw more handwriting in those months than I'd seen in years. They knew what was at stake.

After months of cards and notes and calls and texts, the November elections occurred. For both of those elections, the results were too close to declare. And thus the calls, texts, official mailers, and handwritten mail continued for two more months. By the time the runoff election occurred, incumbents had run campaign ads that were visibly anti-Semitic and racist.

On January 5th, I was wide awake before dawn, too excited about voting to care about missed sleep. I savored my short walk to the polls on that cold, clear day, with the marrow-deep certainty of the results, historic for both Georgia and the region.

Though the results weren't certified for more than a week, by early the next morning, victories were declared: Georgia's first Black senator and first Jewish senator.

And yet, we had only a few hours to enjoy the results, because later in the same day was news of a disgusting, horrifying exercise in white supremacy: the insurrection at the Capitol. I didn't have the words to describe my grief and rage; I still don't. As that event was swept up in the relentless news cycle, I was too far gone to appreciate other changes, like a new president and new Congress.

Through the winter, I stayed in my cotton ball cave,

where so much of the world became muffled, in my often still life. I noticed, though, that I had fewer bewildered ramblings in my home. Thought processing remained slow, but it wasn't a sludgy mess anymore.

My Covid cleavage body still had high temperatures and a high frequency of migraines. But at least my brain felt a bit less in a fog. I finally stopped worrying incessantly about early onset dementia. I wanted to believe I was done with Long Covid. Still moving. Roots crawling and mushrooms rising.

In mid-February, I had what I hope is the worst experience I'll ever have on social media. I awoke early on the weekend, and was surprised at the atypical urge to check my phone. I had maintained my limited time on social media, in order to avoid the many dismissive people there.

Immediately, I saw a series of chilling posts from Stella, asking for help. A man she knew was holding her hostage in her home and threatening to kill both of them.

Early on that quiet morning, I knew she was already dead. That my birthday lunch the previous summer was our last time together. The posts had comments, but I skipped reading them. I called her, desperate to cling to any microscopic shred of hope. As the phone rang and rang, I knew she was gone.

I'd already told myself to re-evaluate all the future I no longer believed was likely. Now, I didn't want any future at all.

I dropped like a stone, and the void swallowed me.

I asked, again, to be devoured. I wanted to be devoured.

I am grief. I am shattered. I will never be whole.

I could have done more.

I want to be gone. Now.

I didn't help.

Please make it be over.

I'm done. I'm complete.

I am the weeping woman. I dwell in the vale of tears. I am the vale of all the tears.

I didn't help. I could have done so much more.

I am gone. Done. Please now.

The void was much more available than sleep, not to mention much more appealing. Being out of the void meant being bombarded with memories of her, as well as rage about who killed her.

Too late, I wished I'd visited her. Or at least had disclosed why I didn't—that I was too sick and too sad to witness all her excitement firsthand. I was envious. I was afraid. I was angry. Despite her reminders, no matter her requests, I never went. And now I never would.

The only comfort I derived was that she always knew I loved her deeply. That I saw her bright, courageous, loving soul. And I always believed in her.

Still, that wasn't enough. After she died, I didn't want to be better. The void was the best option. I didn't feel better, but it didn't matter—in the void, nothing mattered and nothing improved. Getting "better" would entail facing the pain of losing my friend. Pain piled on pain piled on pain piled on pain.

I didn't have the strength. Telling myself that I didn't have to try to feel better was a relief. All the more relief that I didn't even have to *want* to feel better. It was fine not to care. It was fine to give up. After all, that had already been my prevailing sentiment for the previous year. Maybe I would never recover, so there was no point in anything anyway.

Spring began on what I wish were the heels of my grief, but in actuality its depths. I had another round of intense allergy-induced sickness, which made me realize I couldn't accurately call them "childhood" allergies anymore. In the worst bouts of fevers, congestion, more headaches, I could barely think straight. Sleep deprivation continued and migraines raged.

I retreated from wanting a clear head anyway. I wanted any distraction, every distraction, to reduce the incessant ruminations about Stella. I barely noticed wearing the same clothes for days, was hardly moved at my own odor.

My partner, who'd held a flicker of hope for me at the beginning of the year, only to see it extinguished at her death, was again profoundly concerned for my well-being. He knew that things were deeply wrong. Meanwhile, I was steadfast in my avoidance of sharing anything of consequence. I said nothing. I cried while he was in meetings, raged when he wasn't home.

The visions that had soothed me for so many years gave no respite. Knives, meat tenderizers, jackhammers—nothing helped. While I don't collect knives, those in my kitchen are more than enough to do plenty of damage. And if I'd been living alone, I think I would have acted on that ideation. As much as I distanced myself from my partner, his presence, simply by working from home, created a buffer between me and self-harm.

As the pollen cleared, I was ready to go outside, once the air was clearer. I walked as often as possible, always for short distances. He was relieved at my meager capacity. I had little physical stamina, but I was still moving. Kelp swaying, oceans waving.

A leisurely neighborhood stroll with him, meaning a mile (1.6km) on gently sloped pavement, made me short of breath, which justified a streaming evening, with us on the couch. I attributed the constant fatigue and shortness of breath to being out of shape. I'd barely exercised for over a year.

Post allergy season, my partner and I visited a family elder. For many years, she'd had a steady routine of walking in her neighborhood, and we always enjoyed joining her. As usual, we walked every evening. Pre-pandemic, she'd had some health struggles and hospital stays, and as a result, she had slowed her pace and decreased the distance, slightly. So, I had a week of even shorter walks, on flatter terrain.

The contrast was illuminating. By the end of her gentler, slower walk, I wasn't completely exhausted, the way I was at home. But I also wasn't full of energy. I had more energy than my elder, who was in her early nineties at the time. But not by much.

Illuminating, indeed, to have barely more stamina than someone a half-century older. That contrast made the subsequent walks a bit depressing. I'd felt so confident that I'd regain some stamina, but I didn't feel any different.

Just like the previous year, I didn't know how permanent or temporary Long Covid would be. I was mildly hopeful, given that I'd observed some small improvement. I had also connected to online groups of long-haulers, where people constantly shared experiences far more serious than mine: multiple hospitalizations, organ failure, seizures, neurological damage, respiratory impairment, and much worse. So many heartbreaking stories, but also affirmation, commiseration, and support.

Still moving. Hummingbirds thrumming. Bats echoing.

A year before, more than half of the time of my asana practice was for resting between fits of coughing. At this point, the hacking was gone. But I was so quickly short of breath that I needed the same rest time. Bitterly, I admitted that Long Covid was deeper in my body than I had thought.

Concurrently, the void tugged at me, with vaporous spiders—majestic and agile—instead of hands. The gossamer touch of these spiders grabbed multiple points of my skin, pulled in multiple directions. I felt these creatures, saw them, and I also heard them. Soft, sliding tones with their own precise definition, the way spiders walk.

While I had fewer migraines and Covid struggles in 2021, I felt no emotional improvement. If anything, my grief made me feel worse. I was grieving the loss of a dear friend, but also the loss of me, to me.

Often I yielded to the pull, because I desperately craved space away from my grief. Being in the void is effortless. No pain, no fear, no discomfort. No joy, no exuberance, no bliss. Just nothing.

I am gone.

I'm done.

I am nothing.

I am gone. I'm done. I am nothing.

Gone.

Nothing.

Done.

Nothing.

Gone. Done. Nothing.

Nothing. Nothing. Nothing.

This escapism also stayed my hands from slinking into the kitchen to find knives—so I never tested whether actual self-harm could have helped when my flights of fancy didn't.

Outside of the void, I had to contend with another clear recollection from November 2019. Just after I returned from paradise, while still very ill with Covid, Stella had texted me, asking to talk. After a long stretch of not seeing or talking to him at all, in a moment of loneliness, she had agreed to a trip with her abusive coward of an ex-boyfriend.

And yes, he was a coward. Not all cowards are abusers, but all abusers are cowards. I told her what I'd tell anyone in that situation: if you have an abuser in your life, that person is a coward and you deserve better. This is not to downplay cowards as harmless—to the contrary, some cowards are the most dangerous people you can know.

Also, if you're reading this and you are an abuser—I know that you're a coward, even if you've fooled everyone else, even yourself. Get help. Courage is a choice.

So, Stella and I talked. I held space for her fear and shame. She didn't want to confront him with a different choice; she was reluctant to admit to wanting to change her mind. I pointed out the obvious: that she didn't call me because she wanted affirmation. She knew that I would remind her that this was a terrible idea, that I would encourage her to change her plans.

She convinced herself easily. Within fifteen minutes of my phone ringing, she canceled the trip. Her next text: "This is loving me more than being lonely."

Then she thanked me for supporting her without judgement. We ended with "I love you," as usual.

And now she's dead, at the hands of that same man.

I burrowed deeper into my energetic pod of bubble wrap and cotton balls. Sleep eluded me, as that conversation looped ceaselessly, echoing the way a crash of thunder reverberates beyond its sound. Numbing out was far more preferable. I had nightmares; I was constantly nauseous.

When Stella died, I felt the weight of wishing I'd been a better friend. Wishing I'd done more to encourage her to stay away from the abuser. Wishing I'd visited her, wishing I could have overcome my struggles. Wishing I didn't have to hate how much my envy prevented me from trying harder.

I don't believe in saviorism. My mind understands that I couldn't have saved her. But my heart doubts that truth.

I recognize that his friends and loved ones connected with him in meaningful ways, because I've witnessed plenty of statements about what "a really great guy" he was. I find wolves to be magnificent creatures, so I choose not to malign them with a wolf in sheep's clothing metaphor here. Rather, I can state plainly that he was an abuser with all the privileges and concessions that come with being charming, good-looking, and charismatic.

In other words: despite Stella's frequent commentary, over many years to many people, that he was violent and dangerous, those people (not just men) constantly ignored her or told her she was overreacting—one of many enabling patterns in the life of this "really great guy" who ended up being a murderer.

That awful morning, her posts reported that he threatened to kill them both. He followed through on his threat, and at least his death was for the best. I refuse to expend precious energy to mourn him. My mind knows that he suffered beyond measure, that his choices brought plenty of suffering to his loved ones. But in the limits of my humanness, my heart doesn't care.

I hated holding all these thoughts and feelings and energy, so the push/pull with the void continued. I wasn't pleading as much as I did the previous year. But I rarely resisted the gossamer tugs from the spiders with their sliding, precise tones.

Sometimes I could start the exit from the void by echoing Stella's words: *This is loving me more than being lonely.*

Love over loneliness. She is dead, but not gone. Now, she is both further and closer than when alive. She has assured me that I'm forgiven, that in fact there is nothing to forgive.

My mind knows. But my heart struggles to accept that truth.

Time crept along. In early summer, when the collective energy felt very "OMG brunch!", I finally shared about my Long Covid experience. Publicly, in a social media post. Several paragraphs with the main highlights: respiratory issues, migraines, and concerns about permanent brain damage. For many people, that post was how they learned about the existence of Long Covid.[1] I had no interest in appointing myself as a spokesperson or even a representative of Long Covid, but I had a flash of satisfaction to share something meaningful.

Some of the readers were also long-haulers, who, like me, had been suffering in silence. People who, like me, had told no one about their condition. They messaged me to commiserate, ask for advice, thank me for sharing, wish me well in my healing process. For most of them, I was the first person they told. Notably, these people were not close friends. Nor did we have a long history. But I was the rare person who was being real, who didn't insist on positivity and optimism.

---

1   And the preponderance of Long Covid for women: "Why are women more prone to long Covid?" by David Cox. *The Guardian*, 13 June 2021.

Especially on social media, where constant filters and curated feeds have accustomed us to a selective reality.

When you live with chronic illness, when you have a fragile existence with an uncertain future, one of the most toxic things that creates the most erasure is exactly what you tend to encounter most often: people who insist on staying positive, having gratitude, maintaining optimism. All of those sentiments are lovely, but they create harm when people insist on them to the point of ignoring everything else.

For example, to the people who messaged me about Long Covid, I validated their experiences, expressed my sympathy and compassion. I told them not to spend time around people who didn't love and support them. I encouraged them to advocate for themselves. Never did I emphasize an exercise regimen, recommend a supplement plan, or insist on the power of positive thinking.

The rest of 2021, outwardly, passed in the same sort of hazy foggy fuzz as 2020, though for completely different reasons. Love over loneliness was what kept me moving through my katabasis. I often thought about Persephone, whose time in the underworld is delineated, whereas my time, in contrast, I thought might never end.

In December 2021, I had a glimpse of what was possible. In the fall, a community theater accepted my proposal for an art installation and performance, as part of a larger event. I carefully hoarded all my energy to prepare. My partner was a huge help; after long workdays, he decorated a lot of the physical space that I couldn't reach, even with a ladder. And

I napped as often as possible in the preceding weeks.

My installation and performance were about destigma-tizing the body, particularly the menstrual cycle. Among other things, I had menstrual charts on the walls, without that explicit label. Some attendees recognized them, but many people (of any gender) did not. That led to fascinating conversations, which I could tell were rare for a lot of them, even those who had menstrual cycles.

I was unaware that *Dobbs v. Jackson* was making its way through the courts, and that in six months those con-versations, as well as those charts, would feel a lot more dangerous. The court decision certainly demonstrates that far too much of certain bodies is legislated. And, of course, many people—particularly people not white, financially sta-ble, cis women—had already been disenfranchised for a long time before this court decision.

By the end of the performances, I was satisfied with everything. I was clear, present, and engaged, even with all performers and attendees masked. And exhausted, though hopefully only my closest friends could have discerned it. I was very comfortable in the appearance of being a "strong and competent" person. That facade provides a lot of secu-rity, and it's something I've cultivated my entire life. Not to say I'm weak or incompetent—I'm neither. But projecting strength and capability was first for survival, and later as safety.

Those performances didn't shift my experience of Long Covid. In fact, they affirmed my reality: slight exertion required excessive rest. Exertion for that week required the rest of the month to recover. My asana practice slowed. My body cemented again.

By the end of the year, I felt the same as I did at the start. My aerobic capacity remained minimal. Those short, leisurely strolls on gently sloped pavement didn't get any easier, so I never walked longer distances. Those short distances still justified leisurely evenings.

Over the course of the year, I became accustomed to how much recovery was necessary for any exertion or excursion. Two loads of laundry in the same day could be so tiring that I didn't want to shower. Going to the post office might mean that I canceled a phone call with a friend, because it hurt to maintain a conversation.

I did my best to plan carefully and avoid doing too much, but it's impossible to account for all possibilities. The only way to control everything is to do nothing.

Culturally, rest is often regarded as frivolous, while productivity matters above all. I defaulted to the usual masking and hiding, downplaying how much I didn't do. I returned to my earlier script, that I had headaches and I was tired.

I passed another uninspiring anniversary of the illness that had broken my whole life, made my life felt like an endless lull.

What I better understand now—both from my experience and discussions with long-haulers—is that Long Covid aggravates previous or chronic conditions, from fibroids to fibromyalgia and anything else. Already, long-haulers are sharing heartbreaking stories about long term disability or permanent damage. Many people are living the outcomes that I feared. And much worse.

2022

In early 2022, I learned about long-term blockage in the lungs of many long-haulers, that had previously gone undetected.[1] It wasn't accurate to me at the time, but it definitely tracked with my past experience. It also affirmed my understanding that Long Covid didn't stop with the end of my worst coughing fits or heavy brain fog, nearly a year before. I was grateful for the clarity.

I was even more grateful for a shift that felt like a split second, diamond flash on water: after years of struggling to do a minimal postural practice, I needed fifteen minutes on the mat for fifteen minutes of asana. With a clearer mind and more open lungs, I dared hope that thinking and breathing would no longer be difficult. I dared hope for the indeterminate future.

Still moving. Breezes whispering and leaves rustling.

And yet, in my third spring since contracting Covid, I was the sickest I'd been since late 2019: multiple stints

---

1   "Long Covid study finds abnormality in lungs that could explain breathlessness" by Hannah Devlin. *The Guardian*, 29 January 2022.

of several days of intense sinus pressure, bodyache, fever, constant congestion. It hurt to breathe pollen-saturated air outside. Migraines raged. Sleep recessed, like an ebbing tide that never returned.

The highest temperatures of my life were in spring 2022, with consecutive days over 100°F (38°C). I rested, stayed hydrated, did all the home remedies. Results from home Covid tests were negative. After years of avoiding allopathic medicine for Long Covid, I nearly checked myself into urgent care for persistent fever.

As always, these times provided ample space to reflect on pain. Some people are so afraid of pain that they do any type of mental or spiritual contortion to bypass it into fiction or invention. Pain as "unreal." Pain as "disguise." They insist on "high vibes only" and go to spaces that promise perfect peace and ease and relaxation, with not even a brush of discomfort.

That bypassing is a lot of effort. Not to mention that plenty of your life will simply pass by, without you noticing. The human experience often brims with pain. Pain is not a sign that you're doing life wrong. Pain is a sign you're fully alive.

Recognizing pain, acknowledging it fully, allows for personal choice in integration and understanding. Plenty of people see their hardships as something for the best, something from their god, that it all turned out exactly as Divine Will intended. Something they would never change, even if given the chance.

I support those folks. But projecting any perspective onto everyone is harmful. I have zero desire to claim it. So, I'm in no need of reminders or advice or projections that I Just Need To Find The Good And Cultivate Gratitude.

Did the worst of my Long Covid years also have a torrent of spiritual initiations? Unquestionably.

I no longer believe that I'm a burden to my loved ones. I don't doubt all the love in my life.

I have altered my definitions of strength, of toughness. I've released my desire for (the illusion of) hyper-independence.

I recognize the poison of hiding my pain. That in my efforts to spare my loved ones from suffering, I simply brewed a giant batch of poison that I guzzled alone.

I move easily into my vibrational mind, tune in more to vibrational wisdom.

I know love cannot be destroyed. Relationships, sure, sometimes forever. But not love.

Are there other ways to experience those initiations? Abso-fucking-lutely.

Might I have gained these insights without Long Covid? I'll never "know" in an experiential sense, but my answer is nevertheless an emphatic YES.

I have my own relationship with migraines and Long Covid. They are teachers, guides, and even allies. And I project that perspective on no one. These relationships have taken years to cultivate, with ongoing nurturing. That journey is beyond the scope of this book, but those relationships have given me profound insights and deep healing, as well as activated my spiritual gifts.

Pain is pain, just as joy is joy. Pleasure is pleasure. Agony is agony; bliss is bliss; despair is despair; delight is delight.

The universe doesn't require that you believe anything is for the best. Or the worst. If you insist that all hardships are Divine Will in action, that they always turn out for the best, I encourage you to look around the world and consider more deeply.[2]

For those who do notice the world—trust the struggle. The body doesn't lie.

Having spent most of my life living with chronic pain, I recognize the holiness of it, just as everything is sacred. Pain is pain, as I mentioned. Not pleasant. But in whatever capacity—be it anger, grief, dis-ease, or anything else—pain holds both something you love and the violation of it. Being present to pain is the capacity to hold profound love amidst violation or violence.

(Not that the experience actually feels that way in the moment. But that's how I understand it.)

Because pain has purpose. Anger at a friend who makes a mistake that violates your well-being, because you love yourself, your friend, your friendship. Grief at all the injustice in the world, because you cherish children and trees and oceans and rocks and animals and plants and people.

---

2   See also: abuse, sexual assault, chronic illness, disabilities, generational traumas. As a start.

Likewise, joy has purpose, to give capacity for love and celebration, even within a world of ceaseless violation and violence. Among many things, joy provides the energetic and emotional reserves that carry you through pain.

Insisting that pain is fiction only invalidates your lived experience. And then, when another part of your lived experience is scary or intimidating or uncomfortable or even too good to be true, you'll make that happiness into fiction too. Just like pain.

If you're thinking that I'm a spoiled, privileged brat—that a woman with white privilege and a mild case of Long Covid is too wrapped up in her tiny struggle—then yeah, welcome to my thoughts. I hated myself for what I perceived as weakness. That what has been a mild experience of Long Covid—not a mild illness, not at all, but a mild case of LC—has been so debilitating.

I remind myself, though, that denying people's pain and invalidating their lived experience are exactly what alienate them. This dismissal can happen from friends, family, colleagues, and medical professionals. I remember that the more marginalized people are—far more than I—the more likely this happens.

In these years, damn near everything I loved—damn near everything, loved or not—burned down. In this katabasis, I had no assurance of its end, ever.

I also continue to navigate exposure and contagion, which for me are life and death decisions. I'm relying on observations, instinct, and anecdotal evidence to evaluate my elevated risk.

Long Covid has been so debilitating that I haven't believed that I could ever muster the energy to return to a life, and a self, that I recognize. Some days, when I'm aching to do things—write, create art, make plans with friends, have a semblance of a life I recognize—some days, I have both the inspiration and the interest. But I'm rarely able to summon the energy or the will. Days without steady, debilitating pain feel like something in my distant past. Fragile, seahorse memories, perhaps never to be known again.

Not to mention my anxiety in social spaces—the utter discomfort in my rare moments of being in large groups of people. In spaces where people are so delighted to gather again, hug again, laugh again, make eye contact in person again.

Whereas I find myself, all too easily, all too readily, touching the void: fingers brushing smoke, reminding me of my wraith self. This specter can be so near, a psychopomp to the void. The dis-ease rising: stomach roiling, skin crawling, bile rising in my mouth. Disorientation. I don't know how to be or who I am, just that I'm a buzzkill to all the joy and excitement. Poison.

In those spaces, I consider all the hearts beating, blood pulsing, lungs bellowing. The world is still moving, as always, regardless of me. I am still moving in those same ways: my heart beats, my blood pulses, my lungs bellow. And yet I feel as though I'm not even there. Everyone else moves in ways that wraith me does not: joking, hugging, laughing.

Because I need to grieve. Not just have grief, but actually express it. Mainstream culture barely acknowledges the existence of grief, let alone honors the expression of it. Even less so encourages that expression. I need to process my grief by moaning and groaning, ranting and raving, weeping and rending. But also through laughing, through expressing ecstatic joy. Plenty of people want the latter, but bypass the former. I want both, as well as all that is betwixt and between, among and around and about. It's difficult to find spaces that truly welcome and encourage everything.

Though some people are willing to comfort me when I'm in pain, I've witnessed others moving away. Especially over time. It's one thing to comfort me when I'm having a tough day. But what about when every day is tough, for years? A lot of people want to be supportive, but are also overwhelmed by my situation, one without a happy resolution or even a hopeful arc.

And I sympathize. I've had that resistance and discomfort too. Holding space in those moments is intense. But without people holding space in those moments, I feel wrong—the same way I felt wrong when I was crying in frustration and pain at the meditation retreat. Even though nothing is actually wrong with me.

In those moments, I feel mySelf slither to smoke, slide into the void. Noises fade, no longer making my skin ache. I worry that the wraith me is disruptive. That I'm poison. But I also know that doesn't matter. I'm gone to where nothing matters. The world is still moving, but I cannot, in those moments. I descend to nothing, for nothing.

Eventually, I return. Still moving.

Despite my criticisms, I do believe in hope, when it's devoid of the residue of bypassing. I recognize the power of hope, the power of imagination to believe beyond what's immediately present.

Concurrently, I recognize that sometimes, not clinging to hope allows me to be fully present. For the umpteenth time, I allow hopelessness to exist too. I don't shame mySelf when I lack the desire to heal.

Because healing, in my experience, always induces deeper pain along the journey. So I ponder, languidly, the merits of remaining in my current levels of pain. As opposed to arousing even more pain, for the sake of healing the current pain.

In 2020 and 2021, I descended into the underworld, with no certainty of ever ascending. Slowly, slowly, in glacial timing, I've clawed my way upward. Like Persephone, I know that I will, from time to time, return. Though I hope—truly, sincerely hope—that my chthonic returns will not nearly be as precise or as long as hers.

Because I'm realistic, I can be cynical as I can be about the world, which is a messy, difficult place, full of violence and injustice. And because I'm realistic, I believe that our purpose here is to love each other. That joy, bliss, awe, and wonder are our natural, intrinsic states.

Emphasis on natural and intrinsic. You don't have to be a sweepstakes winner; you need only witness the world.

The colors at twilight. Morning birdsong. The sound of wind singing through trees. The sight of trees dancing in that windsong. The feel of silky smooth fabric on the skin. The warmth of fuzzy socks. A baby's laughter. The colors and shapes of clouds.

The world offers endless moments to savor, marvel, and delight at beauty, mystery, and love. I don't want to squander or miss these moments. We exist in that joy, though, not by repeated denial of part of ourselves, denial about the injustices in the world, or denial of our primal experiences, including pain. We live in that bliss and wonder by honoring our totality of experience.

Most of 2022 progressed with less of the foggy haze of previous years, though migraines and fevers persisted with much more frequency than I wanted. Two days a week, give or take, were consumed by pain.[3] Likewise, my mind remained fuzzy. I frequently struggled to find my words, so when I couldn't remember "dishwasher" or "shoelaces," I panicked inside.

Slowly, though, I have begun to be someone familiar. In early summer, enough of a gap between migraines emerged that I started to sleep better. I didn't sleep as long as I liked, not near enough, because lying down for long stretches of

---

3   If you don't have a chronic illness, that might not seem like much time. But imagine if every weekend, plus random additional days, of an entire year was lost to headaches, fevers, and disrupted sleep. And the weekdays were constantly impacted by the pain and sleep deprivation.

time was often painful. Nonetheless, for the first time in years, I had fairly consistent, uninterrupted sleep.

As I finally rested, I found more stamina, for the first time since autumn 2019. Fewer rest gaps in a longer asana practice, longer walks without fatigue. I had energetic stamina—I wanted to make art, be more social, learn new things. I wanted to talk to my partner in more than monosyllables.

Over the moon cycles, my menstrual cycle changed as well. In 2020 and 2021, I thought perimenopause might be imminent. I mean, I gained a lot of grey hair in a short span of time. Instead, my cycle became less haywire.

Still moving. Octopi wandering and spiders weaving.

And yet, I struggled to establish a more tactile life. I didn't know who I am/was or what to do with mySelf. I wasn't actively sick, but I didn't actually feel better. The incessant migraines were gone, but I was still consumed by dis-ease, by emotional illness.

I remembered those occasional fantasies, just two years prior, of my complete certainty that I'd feel amazing once I was no longer sick. Even I, with my extensive experience of pain and illness, was blissfully ignorant that not being sick is not equal to being well.

In the fall, I attended a friend's backyard birthday gathering. I barely knew any of the guests, so I mostly listened and observed. Which was good, as holding conversations with strangers tired me easily. Not to mention I didn't have much capacity for conversation, even if I wanted it. Which I most assuredly did not.

I don't recall when or how the group conversation turned to Long Covid. I was listening and observing, from an energetic distance. Maybe one person knew a long-hauler, or the long-hauler was a friend of a friend. Anyway, people started joking about Long Covid. Namely, that it was a great excuse for a sick day from work: "Y'know, you have a headache. Or you feel groggy from a few late nights. Just tell your boss that you have Long Covid! Totally reasonable."

What a pivot, right? Not the usual pandemic pivot of people changing their lifestyle and/or profession, but the pivot of attitudes in a short span. Just two years before, we all lived in the bombardment of deniers and conspiracies. Now, people joked heartily in their belief of the existence of the illness. And while I doubt that any of these folks were Covid deniers, these kinds of jokes are a sort of denial.

I get that long-haulers weren't supposed to be the punchline. But that dismissiveness made us into punchlines anyway. At that moment, the illness and the jokes were close enough that people's laughs landed directly on me.

I was too gobsmacked to counter anyone's statements. Or identify myself as a long-hauler. Or even point out that these same jokes about different illnesses—cancer, MS, heart disease—are completely inappropriate. Maybe if I'd known more people, I would have said something. But in that moment, I was grateful to be sitting mostly in the dark, blinking back tears and trying to quell the lump in my throat—not so dissimilar from sitting at the meditation retreat, while another person claimed I didn't know my own experience. I left the party shortly thereafter, without saying anything else. I never told the host, as I didn't want to cause embarrassment to anyone, including me.

After years of feeling like a stranger, I found something familiar. Miserably familiar, but something I recognized. In that moment by the fire pit, I would have happily disappeared into the embers, the way I used to want to disappear into my books when I was constantly crying in front of my bookshelf.

Which was the opposite of what I'd been craving. For years, I'd wanted to find the pre-pandemic me. She was ever more distant, like a sight receding in a rearview mirror. The person who laughed readily, relished physical activity, sustained attention on meaningful things.

I had resisted my changeling self. But I was finally willing to notice who she is, at present.

She still sees a stranger in the mirror and still avoids photos. She still has frequent migraines. She still can't lie down for long stretches of time.

For the last few months, her right shoulder and upper arm hurt so much that she winces every time she lifts that arm. Some days the shoulder granite feels like gravel, other days like a monadnock.

She still freaks out inside whenever her mind sputters, which is often. The seahorses in her brain don't readily move memory from short to longer tem. She rarely understands instructions or requests on the first pass. She is forgetful. When a friend mentions their lunch date last week, she realizes she'd forgotten—the lunch date, the restaurant, the food—until the friend's remark.

Sometimes a big day is finishing two loads of laundry. Other times a big day is sending two emails.

For the record, she does remember her Social Security number again.

Nevertheless, I realize I can accept this familiar-and-changeling self. I don't fully know her or understand her. But I do know she's no less false than the existence of pain or bliss.

I am acutely aware that my current capacity is not unlike a knife edge, narrow and precarious. It's all too easy to overstep and push beyond what's sustainable in a given day, in a given week. Realistically, overburdening such a limited capacity is inevitable. Life happens. Too much time in a grocery store—a place that's always been overstimulating for me—can make me too tired to complete the one other errand (like returning a library book) before I need to go home to rest. A social dinner requires more time to sleep in the next morning, or maybe extra naps for the rest of the week.

All this down time gives a lot of space for the classic existential questions. Why am I here, now? After so many others have died, when so many others have suffered more? Why me, and not Stella, who had a vibrant life, who brought so much healing to the world? I wanted to stop breathing so many times—I begged to stop breathing, so many times. Living in a country awash in the blood of mass shootings, why have I survived?

After spending so much time begging for death, it was never granted to me.

I've surrendered to what many people have realized throughout human history—that on this plane of existence, satisfactory explanations don't exist. These answers can't be known or understood because they can't contort into the limitations of human understanding.

I used to cling to "getting better"—to the day when I'd start thinking clearly and breathing easily. That I'd feel so amazing. Breathing and thinking are a big improvement for me, but those alone are not much of a life. Now that I do think and breathe easily, I'm definitely not upholding my side of my proposed bargain, of being clear and steadfast and perfect.

Regardless of how I define a recovery from Long Covid, whether I ever reach a full recovery—what do I do in this body, in this time?

People often use the caterpillar-to-butterfly metaphor for a healing journey. In those descriptions, the chrysalis is usually a passing phase, a still, quiet thing. Really, though, that's far from accurate. The cocoon is actually the wildest stage, an oozy, slimy space wherein a creature turns to goo and reforms in a different body with wings. Metamorphosis, like healing, is not passive and quiet.

Perhaps I just need to adjust my metaphor to a moth, a more chthonic creature.

Either way, that oozy, gooey, slimy time is necessary. And what emerges is beautiful. On my good days, I strive to make the best of my phlegmy, messy, slimy time. My years of what's been a phlegmy, messy, slimy cocoon.

Still moving, I s'pose, will carry me to something. Clinging for answers seems more futile than clinging to recovery.

I feel I must be a burden to the world, and yet the world has never shown me anything of that nature. Everything is connected. The trees breathe; I breathe. The world keeps showing me light diamonding on water and flowers gulping light. Still moving.

An invitation, if acknowledged. Encouragement, if received.

Invitation and encouragement to recognize all these moments of remembering, of connecting to all that's moving. To attune to beauty, mystery, joy. To remember that Stella's right—to choose love over loneliness.

We humans can experience the depths of sorrow, the worst losses. And the soaring triumphs, the outrageous joys. Plus all the other colors and textures and nuances betwixt and between, among and around and about. By now, surely it's no surprise that I dismiss the idea that life "should" be easy all the time. Equally, though, I disagree with the assertion that life is only pain. We can experience everything; we are created to experience everything. We are meant to experience everything.

After years of masking my struggle—and nearly all of my life masking neurodivergence and chronic illness—I remind mySelf of wisdom from Kahlil Gibrain: "Your joy is your sorrow unmasked." For years, I didn't understand what that meant. Though certainly it's related to another part of the same work: "The deeper that sorrow carves into your being, the more joy you can contain."

Lest you think that I'm advocating for something overly simplistic, like "more pain = more love!", I understand his definition as it relates to capacity.

Meaning that your capacity to feel pain is actually the same as your capacity to feel love. Your willingness to feel pain is actually the same as your willingness to feel love. Furthermore, that pain allows, even creates, depths for love. Mind you, not love as a saccharine sentiment, but the courageous choice to feel the totality of your own experience.

Pain and grief and healing—labyrinths that at times masquerade as mazes. Instead of the usual low hedges or rocks of a labyrinth, the boundaries are tall, like a maze. Along the way, you bump into walls, stumble over corners, pass along turns that, at first, seem like dead ends. As labyrinths do, the path loops around on itself, a multidimensional ouroboros.

And if you continue along this labyrinth of pain or grief or healing, you eventually reach the center—the core of your heart.

…only to find it labyrinths further, spiraling into yet unencountered layers in the depths of love.

Which offers the choice to trust my changeling self, to rely on my guides, to stay curious with the universe and with this unfathomable, wild, human incarnation.

To remain steadfast with the willingness to meander the labyrinthine course of love, even in times of doubt. When the labyrinth feels more like a cruel maze of trapdoors and hazards and dead ends, to recognize the center is not a reward of puppies and warm fuzzies and no more problems, but actually the opportunity to experience the universe more fully.

As a summer child, I have always appreciated the reflection from Albert Camus about the season: "In the depths of winter, I finally learned that within me there lay an invincible summer." That's the closest explanation for my choice of still moving, even when my mind rationalized reasons to stop. Somewhere, like lightning flashing and auroras blazing, was the fiery unwillingness to quit, regardless of its source.

Through my long-hauler experience, I have found an invincible spring. This invincible spring is both season and source: a season that blooms at any time, as well as a source that emerges all the time.

The Persephone myth was among the first Greek myths I ever learned. Since myths skim over details, I have always loved to create my own. In my imagining, Persephone holds the ripened-to-the-point-of-bruised pomegranate, just after realizing the implication of eating the seeds. Her hands quiver. The seeds glisten. Overcome with emotion, she crushes the fruit, red flowing between her fingers and down her arms.

Maybe she's actually holding her heart. Pulsing, glistening. Bleeding through her crushing fingers.

Persephone—the goddess of spring, the queen of the

underworld. Not just witnessing her own heartbreak, but willing to participate in the destruction. Not life or death. Life and death. Both.

She crushes that fruited, bleeding heart and ascends to initiate the spring.

That season, then, connects to the infinite well. Spring as season and source, capable of quenching the unquenchable.[4] The invincible spring both within me and beyond me—indefatigable, indomitable, inevitable.

I do know that I must be, day to day, moment to moment, breath to breath, this invincible spring –

Still moving.

---

4   "Many waters cannot quench love, nor the floods drown it."
     ~ Song of Songs 8:7

afterwords

Some people say the best art is timeless. However good or not, this is a work clearly embedded in time, born out of a specific time. A specific collective time, but also a specific personal epoch. I hope that this work supports you towards deeper reflections and more meaningful connections.

I know humans will unpack this pandemic, these years, for generations. The collective experience that manifested in countless ways, with innumerable consequences and impacts.

As I've frequently described, Covid has more implications than a typical flu. Please take that as a gentle reminder to take care of yourself and others.

I wrote this book before the "end"—if one ever exists— to my long-hauler experience. Which is to acknowledge and affirm that I'm still refining my understanding of my own experience. Moreover, I want to emphasize again that I've had a mild case of Long Covid. No hospitalizations, no medications, nothing catastrophic like seizures or organ failure. And yet, navigating contagion and exposure remain life and death choices.

My focus in 2023 was rebuilding, re-establishing a life. Preferably one I recognize, but maybe not. I've been too sick to be picky, and for now I'll settle for anything better than my worst of Long Covid. No preference, so much as wanting my identity not to be primarily that of a sick person.

It's going ok, I suppose. I don't have migraines all the time, though any significant experience out of my home often means I have a migraine the next day. Everything exhausts me. The knife edge of my capacity is even narrower than I first understood. I'm slightly better at balancing on it, but not much.

Recently, I tucked a basket of groceries under a table of the market, for the sake of conserving energy so I could walk down the crowded aisle. I've done this for years. Moments later, after picking up another item, I didn't see the basket where I'd left it. Immediately, I was irate at the person who stole it or the employee who moved it. Cursing freely under my breath, I repeated my entire shopping list into a new basket.

Not until I returned home did I realize that I'd remembered incorrectly where I'd left the basket. I'd walked right by it and didn't question the reflex to blame something external. I had ample time in which I didn't remember what I'd just done. Ample time that I didn't question my own memory.

In twenty years of grocery shopping for myself (because I cooked nearly all the food I ate), even in very stressful times, I never, ever had something like this happen. Sure, there's a first time for everything. And there's the lingering concern how much of my brain is permanently altered.

Because I have frequent moments when I wonder the latter. My whole life, I've loved learning and studying. I am ravenously curious; I see connections in everything. Even without letters after my name or extensive higher education, I have constantly enrolled in classes and courses and workshops, almost without interruption, since my formal education ended.

These days, I find that I dread learning new things. I am easily confused, often on the first step. I need someone else present to keep me from freezing before I begin. But even if I persevere, I rarely retain what I've learned. Those fragile seahorses are easily overwhelmed by the currents of information, whether it's something on a computer or chords on an instrument.

Not surprisingly, I detest this change. Worse than that, though, this change is deeply triggering. The moments of forgetting, or struggling to start, make me worry that my brain will always be broken.

As you've read, I have often understood my case of Long Covid retroactively, and that story continues, beyond the 2019-2022 scope of this book. For example, in summer 2023 I found an article that introduced me to PEM, the debilitating fatigue that often accompanies Long Covid, which, y'know, describes my entire experience.[1]

In online discussions with other long-haulers, deper-

---

1   "Fatigue can shatter a person" by Ed Yong. *The Atlantic*, 27 July 2023. This article addresses PEM (post-exertional malaise) in the context of both Long Covid and ME/CFS (Chronic Fatigue Syndrome).

sonalization and derealization are common topics. The descriptors are new to me, but not the experiences. I am still learning that what has felt singular is actually very common.

I have mentioned that much of my long-hauler experience holds true for the experience of living with chronic conditions. It's also impossible for one person's experience to be universal. I believe in honoring the totality of people's lived experiences, which means individuals claiming and defining themselves.

For the long-haulers – this journey can make you want to give up, all the time. I endured a lot of it not just day by day, but often hour by hour, if not breath by breath. Don't make my mistakes and isolate yourself. If you have anyone lingering in your life who's still denying this disease, I hope you can hold a better space for yourself, with loving, supportive people.

For everyone else – please give people grace. Honor their experiences; believe them. Help them find support that's actually meaningful to them, not something that soothes your own reactions.[2]

People often ask me how to support long-haulers or those with chronic illness. While they have good intentions, many

---

2 Important tangent: This applies not just to long-haulers or people with chronic illnesses; this is true for humans. When people tell you about themselves, believe them. Especially if they're sharing life experiences you can't have. For example, if they are BIPOC and you're not, believe them. If they're LGBTQIA+ and you're not, believe them. Believe what's beyond your perspective.

of them, in my observation, lack the capacity that's truly needed. They are uncomfortable with the intensity of the pain, the duration of the pain.

That discomfort is understandable and reasonable. But it tends to make people default to optimism: they say to stay positive and have gratitude. The attempts to comfort ultimately land as dismissal. Those responses often feel like diminishment, like erasure. We're told that our lived experiences aren't real, or maybe just exaggerated. All my life, doctors and other medical professionals have told me that I'm imagining or exaggerating my pain. Only once has a medical professional believed my account of my own life.

People who don't have chronic conditions might not know how much it helps to have someone listen to you, believe you, and honor your pain. Too often, people think they have to DO something, that action matters more than anything else. Whereas those of us who are afraid to be honest, because the world dismisses our pain, really need people to BE with us.

Being present is more supportive than many people realize. But being present can feel difficult. Or uncomfortable. Because being present acknowledges that an easy fix might not exist. Being present acknowledges that pithy words of wisdom might not change anything.

Being present can feel futile.

The irony, though, is that this thing that might feel like nothing is actually something deeply meaningful. And so simple as to be easy, once you release expectations of what (you think) people need. Not an easy fix, but definitely readily available support.

Which is essential, because self-harm and suicide are epidemic. Being able to hold space for pain is how we take care of each other and heal. And people with chronic illness are far from the only ones suffering. Marginalized people are among the highest likelihood for self-harm and suicide. They need affirmation and care.

And don't forget the "strong" or "happy" people, who so frequently support others, many of whom could never imagine that their strong, confident, capable friends also frequently need support.

When a "strong" person comes to you in a crisis of exhaustion or fatigue or despair, that person is already BEYOND the breaking point. Already. Telling people to be hopeful, that they're strong enough to handle their struggle, invalidates their pain.

If you're well-intentioned but also can't be in the discomfort of these moments—I promise that your friends not only know, but I also promise, I swear, emphatically, that they won't come to you in times of despair or crisis. Which is, of course, when we most want to care for our loved ones.

The capacity to be present with pain is something learned. If you want to learn, start studying. Tell your loved ones that you want to cultivate this ability. Tell your loved ones you love them. Make it weird. The learning goes faster.

One of my favorite quotes is from (oft-maligned) Henry David Thoreau: "Perhaps it seemed to me that I had several more lives to live, and could not spare any more time for that one." That has repeatedly held true for me. Observing my life now, it's clear that parts of me have died. The difference from all the deaths before is that I'd like some of these parts to continue living. So I look to rebirth, and trust emergence.

Emergence, in its original meaning, by the way, meant "unforeseen occurrence." Another familiar word has the same root: emergency. For my Long Covid experience, they weave together perfectly.

Long-hauler life is still spiraling. At times I recognize that I'm in the pain that's the relief of the greater pain. But it still hurts. I'm still drinking from the invincible spring, still being the invincible spring.

In those currents, sometimes I wonder whether the invincible spring has any connection to the void. If they are cosmic kin of sorts, in a multidimensional, partial overlap. Complement, counterpoint, counterpart.

Maybe I'll find you in those surging depths sometime.

I'm glad we're here. You are a blessing. Take exquisite care. I love you.

S.

resources

This section is primarily focused on the US, where I live, and on Long Covid. It is not intended to be comprehensive about Covid, the pandemic, the responses to the pandemic, diagnosis, medical treatment, or anything else.

Relevant definitions

All links accessed 19 July 2023.

epidemic: temporary prevalence of a disease; rapid spread or increase in occurrence of something https://www.dictionary.com/browse/epidemic

pandemic: disease prevalent in an entire country, continent, or the entire world https://www.dictionary.com/browse/pandemic

endemic: settled to a consistent rate of occurrence https://www.dictionary.com/browse/endemic

COVID-19: infectious disease caused by the SARS-CoV-2 virus, frequently manifesting as mild to moderate respiratory illness, that can cause more serious illness or death https://www.who.int/health-topics/coronavirus#tab=tab_1

Long COVID: continuation of illness or development of new symptoms
  3 months after initial infection, lasting at least 2 months with no
  other explanation
  https://www.who.int/europe/news-room/fact-sheets/item/
  post-covid-19-condition#:~:text=It%20is%20defined%20as%20
  the,months%20with%20no%20other%20explanation.

Text note: Because official formatting above (COVID-19 and Long
  COVID) were established after the start of the pandemic, resources
  and works cited show many variations (long Covid, long COVID,
  etc). For the sake of reducing eye fatigue, I have deviated from official
  formatting, using "Covid" and "Long Covid."

Useful overview of the emergence of Long Covid: "How and why
  patients made Long Covid" by Felicity Callard & Elisa Perego.
  National Library of Medicine, January 2021.
  https://www.ncbi.nlm.nih.gov/pmc/articles/PMC7539940/

Suicide & Crisis Hotline & Website in the US: 988 This hotline and
  website have specific resources for Black mental health, indigenous
  populations, veterans, LGBTQ+, attempt survivors, loss survivors,
  neurodivergents, Covid, en español, and more. This resource is also
  useful education for those who want to support their loved ones.
  https://988lifeline.org

Works cited in text

in order of appearance:

"Italy's health system at limit in virus-struck Lombary" by Winfield &
Frances D'Emilio. *Associated Press*, 3 March 2020. https://apnews.com/
article/837274f1bab9af1aab12f1b9481b2d62 Accessed 19 July 2023.

"The Extraordinary Decisions Facing Italian Doctors" by Yascha Mount.
The Atlantic, 11 March 2020. https://www.theatlantic.com/ideas/
archive/2020/03/who-gets-hospital-bed/607807/ Accessed
19 July 2023.

"Special Report: 'All is well'. In Italy, triage and lies for virus patients" by
Emilio Parodi, Silvia Aloisi, & Pamela Barbaglia. *Reuters*, 16 March
2020. https://www.reuters.com/article/s-health-coronavirus-italy-
ethics-speci/special-report-all-is-well-in-italy-triage-and-lies-for-
virus-patients-idUSKBN2133KG Accessed 19 July 2023.

"Ethical Anguish in a Time of COVID-19" by Joel Shurkin.*Inside Science*,
27 March 2020. https://www.insidescience.org/news/ethical-
anguish-time-covid-19 Accessed 19 July 2023.

"Native American health center asked for COVID-19 supplies. It got
body bags instead." by Erik Ortiz. *NBC News*, 6 May 2020.
https://www.nbcnews.com/news/us-news/native-american-health-
center-asked-covid-19-supplies-they-got-n1200246
Accessed 19 July 2023.

"COVID-19 can last for several months" by Ed Yong.*The Atlantic*, 4 June
2020. https://www.theatlantic.com/health/archive/2020/06/
covid-19-coronavirus-longterm-symptoms-months/612679/
Accessed 19 July 2023.

"Long-haulers are redefining COVID-19" by Ed Yong. *The Atlantic*,
19 August 2020. https://www.theatlantic.com/health/archive/
2020/08/long-haulers-covid-19-recognition-support-groups-
symptoms/615382/ Accessed 19 July 2023.

"Why are women more prone to long Covid?" by David Cox.
The Guardian, 13 June 2021. https://www.theguardian.com/society/
2021/jun/13/why-are-women-more-prone-to-long-covid
Accessed 19 July 2023.

"Long Covid study finds abnormality in lungs that could explain
breathlessness" by Hannah Devlin. *The Guardian*, 29 January 2022.
https://www.theguardian.com/society/2022/jan/29/long-covid-
study-finds-abnormality-in-lungs-that-could-explain-breathlessness
Accessed 19 July 2023.

"Fatigue can shatter a person" by Ed Yong. *The Atlantic*, 27 July 2023.
https://www.theatlantic.com/health/archive/2023/07/chronic-
fatigue-long-covid-symptoms/674834/ Accessed 27 July 2023.

Selected Timeline

All links accessed 19 July 2023.

2020 - January 20

United States confirms its first case of Covid to the World Health Organization (WHO). https://www.cdc.gov/museum/timeline/covid19.html#:~:text=January%2020%2C%202020,respond%20to%20the%20emerging%20outbreak.

2020 - January 30

WHO releases statement that novel coronavirus (2019-nCoV) is a public Health Emergency of International Concern (PHEIC). https://www.who.int/news-room/detail/30-01-2020-statement-on-the-second-meeting-of-the-international-health-regulations-(2005)-emergency-committee-regarding-the-outbreak-of-novel-coronavirus-(2019-ncov)

2020 - March 11

WHO declares COVID-19 a pandemic. https://www.who.int/director-general/speeches/detail/who-director-generals-opening-remarks-at-the-media-briefing-on-covid-19---11-march-2020

2020 - late March

First lockdowns/shelter in place begin in many countries and in ten US states. In the US, all of them end no later than mid June. https://en.wikipedia.org/wiki/COVID-19_lockdowns#Table_of_pandemic_lockdowns

2020 - May 20

First mention of Long Covid on Twitter, with #LongCovid. https://twitter.com/elisaperego78/status/1263172084055838721?s=20

2020 - May 26

New York City uses refrigerated trucks as makeshift morgues, for the first time since 9/11. https://www.cnn.com/2020/03/26/us/makeshift-morgues-coronavirus-new-york/index.html

2020 - July 10

First announcement in medical literature about Long Covid. https://blogs.bmj.com/bmj/2020/07/10/patients-experiences-of-long-covid-are-missing-from-the-nhs-narrative/

2020 - August 21

WHO first mentions Long Covid. https://www.who.int/docs/default-source/coronaviruse/transcripts/covid-19-virtual-press-conference---21-august.pdf?sfvrsn=ada7ae85_0

2020 - December 14

First medical announcement of what became the first of several Covid variants. On date of access, the source included variants in 2020, 2021, 2022, and 2023. https://www.who.int/publications/m/item/historical-working-definitions-and-primary-actions-for-sars-cov-2-variants

2021 - May 7

In New York City, 750 bodies remain in "long term temporary storage" (refrigerated trucks used as makeshift morgues). https://www.cnn.com/2021/05/07/us/new-york-coronavirus-victims-refrigerated-trucks/index.html

2021 - October 6

WHO establishes a definition of Long Covid. https://www.who.int/publications/i/item/WHO-2019-nCoV-Post_COVID-19_condition-Clinical_case_definition-2021.1

2023 - May 5

WHO declares end to Covid as a global health emergency. https://www.reuters.com/business/healthcare-pharmaceuticals/covid-is-no-longer-global-health-emergency-who-2023-05-05/

acknowledgements

Many people, directly or indirectly, specifically or generally, have encouraged and reminded me who I am. We humans exist in relationship, so much so that I could never properly acknowledge every person who's supported the existence of this work. I don't believe in "self-made" people. "Self-made" success is just a fallacy (among many) of rugged individualism, which is itself settler fantasy. And while this isn't a journal for this purpose, I have a lot of gratitude to express.

The seeds of this book were planted by the curious, compassionate people who asked about my experience, inquired about my health, and wished me well. Thank you for asking. Hopefully by now readers know how much that presence means.

When I started writing, I thought the attempt was pure folly. Thus, to the readers of the very, very rough early drafts: Thank you. Y'all's encouragement is why I continued.

For everyone else: Please don't forget to encourage artists and creatives, of any age and any ability. Lack of encouragement is often what keeps art unrealized.[3]

I wrote this book because eventually I was able to give words to an experience I hadn't wanted to articulate. And yet, those words are still too raw to speak. All the people who know the details, many of whom have discussed them with me—none of them first learned in a conversation. Everyone—my closest friends and family, my partner— everyone first learned through the words you've just read. No one has ever learned because I actually *told* them, in my spoken words.

Maybe one day. Maybe never.

To the people who read various, and sometimes multiple, drafts of this work and provided vital feedback, poignant insights, and meticulous proofreading, I can't thank you enough. I wouldn't have completed this without your help.

To the generous and experienced professionals in editing and publishing, who kindly shared unabashed and wise perspectives, thank you for your advice in managing the many aspects of self-publishing.

This book wouldn't be nearly as good without the keen observations, thoughtful suggestions, and generous encour-

---

3   Regarding the creative process: I need not acknowledge artificial (so-called) intelligence. This is not to debate the validity of AI or hate on those who use it. But while we collectively negotiate the best practices around this tool, I think that transparency about using it is warranted. (I mean, LOL, my Long Covid brain can't handle learning these things anyways. Maybe one day.) So, to be clear about this book: at no point did I use any bots to generate words. I hired humans to do the work beyond my skill set.

agement of Paula, my editor. All the remaining mistakes are mine.

Twilight, I would never understand my past and my present nearly as well without your insights. Thank you for your patience and generosity in sharing your wisdom.

Though we've never met, I'm grateful to Ed Yong, for his dedication to reporting about Long Covid. His work gave me invaluable information and affirmation, without which I never could have navigated my experience.

We've also never met, but I am grateful to Tricia Hersey and The Nap Ministry, for her wisdom and dedication. Those lessons have completely changed my life.

I'm grateful to JL Schnabel, whose artistry has helped me process my grief and hold my own chthonic spaces.

To the many long-haulers I've encountered, I'm both grieving for us and grateful that we can connect and support each other. You have validation, wisdom, and encouragement that no one else can provide.

To the generous lineage holders and teachers who have shared life-sustaining and life-saving practices and wisdom—these are reasons and ways I am still moving. Thank you for your integrity and commitment to consciousness.

To my ancestors, guides, allies, and teachers, thank you for the blessings, lessons, and paths to healing.

To the more-than-human world, thank you for being examples, teachers, and medicine.

Laney, I would have had an even rougher start without you sharing your beautiful, nourishing home space. Thank you for helping me when I had nowhere else to go.

Ember C. Marvela, you told me that draft three was perfect and you wouldn't change a thing. While I will never agree, I love you for saying it. I'm grateful for all the encouragement from you and Rosa.

SK, thank you for always seeing my joy all these years. When I lost it, you brought me back to mySelf.

Jennifer, you threw a lifeline into the void, and turned the tide.

To my sibling, you've always been constant, unwavering support and I never take it for granted. Your willingness to read and discuss made this book much better. Your faith sustained me when I didn't believe in my own work.

To my partner, who understands nearly all and loves all, unconditionally, who makes the unfathomable into reality— you made it possible to write this book. More than that, you made it possible that I'd live to the point of being able to write it. Thank you for loving me and never giving up. Every breath with you is a gift.

I wrote this book because I wanted to channel what could have been an endless scream into blessings. So that's how I want to close:

We're here to love each other. Joy, bliss, awe, and wonder are our natural, intrinsic states. May we all recognize the depths of interconnection and their profound potential for healing. May you be safe, radiant, and blissful—awash in oceans of blessings. And when life feels seasonless, may you find your connection to the invincible spring, with the support of those who love you.

Thank you for being here. Thank you for being. Live life, love life, live love.

S.
autumn 2023

Milton Keynes UK
Ingram Content Group UK Ltd.
UKHW041048201123
432906UK00004B/111

9 798989 353903